Twayne's United States Authors Series

EDITOR OF THIS VOLUME

David J. Nordloh

Indiana University, Bloomington

Emma Lazarus

TUSAS 353

Emma Lazarus

EMMA LAZARUS

By DAN VOGEL

Jerusalem College for Women
Israel

TWAYNE PUBLISHERS

A DIVISION OF G. K. HALL & CO., BOSTON

Published in 1980 by Twayne Publishers,
A Division of G. K. Hall & Co.
All Rights Reserved

Printed on permanent/durable acid-free paper and bound
in the United States of America

First Printing

Library of Congress Cataloging in Publication Data

Vogel, Dan.
Emma Lazarus.

(Twayne's United States authors series; TUSAS 353)
Bibliography: p. 174–78
Includes index.
1. Lazarus, Emma, 1849–1887.
PS2234.V6   811′.4   79-18875
ISBN 0-8057-7233-2

For Simeon, Mindy, and Jeremy

Contents

About the Author

Dan Vogel has been professor of English at the Michlalah-Jerusalem College for Women since 1973. He received his Ph. D. degree from New York University in 1956 and has taught at Rutgers, City University of New York, St. Johns (New York), Yeshiva University, and Stern College. He has published essays on Emerson, Hawthorne, Melville, Steinbeck, and Bellow, as well as genre studies on American-Jewish literature and "journey" literature in *College English*, *Nineteenth-century Fiction*, *Criticism*, *Nathaniel Hawthorne Journal*, *Tradition*, and *Emerson Society Quarterly*. His book on American tragic writing, *The Three Masks of American Tragedy*, was published in 1974 by Louisiana State University Press. He is now at work on a book dealing with the application of critical theory to the teaching of literature. Essays on the English-language reading program in Israeli high schools have appeared in *English Teachers Manual* (Ministry of Education) in 1975 and 1979.

Preface

Emma Lazarus began her career as a teen-age poetess of genteel, sentimental sighs inspired by Greek mythology and continental Romanticism. What attracted more interest in her than her talent must have warranted in those days was the fact that Emma Lazarus was a Jewess, a curiosity, as Alfred Kazin has pointed out.[1] Those poems, however, were not the source of her authentic literary reputation. Later in life she turned to Jewish themes, and when she died at the age of thirty-eight, E. C. Stedman, a literary critic of some contemporary importance, said of her:

Her writings, especially her poetry . . . . changed in later years from its early reflection of the Grecian ideals and took on a lyrical and veritably Hebraic fire and imagination . . . . There was a contagious inspiration in her Semitic ardor, her satire, wrath, and exaltation.[2]

It is these later poems that have received the accolades of such later critics as George F. Whicher as well. Professor Whicher once differentiated between writers "whose only motives were literary" and those inspired by "personal and ancestral ties with Europe." The latter "are easily distinguishable by reason of their firmness, poise, and point." His chief illustration is the work of Emma Lazarus. Her early verses, he points out, were "written under the spell of Emerson," but "when the wrongs of her people fired her indignation . . . the desire to be heard stripped her verse of its finespun elaboration and brought to her lips the majestic accents of a racial past. . . . The breath of a great cause blew through her verse with tonic effect." [3]

With Emma Lazarus, the great ethnic contribution of native Jewish literature to American letters had begun. But her life and work have greater importance than merely being "first." She exemplified the experience of a minority writer in democratic America, dangling between assimilation into the general culture and adherence to the call of the ancient race. She is a real-life anticipation of the heroes of later American Jewish fiction, the heroes of Abraham Cahan and Ludwig Lewisohn, of Bernard Malamud, Philip Roth, and Saul Bellow. Indeed, she even presaged the spiritual odyssey of some of those authors!

In view of the critical acclaim of the Jewish poems of the last six years of her life, this book will attempt to trace biographically and critically how she got there. After a quick survey of her life, times, and relations with other literati, it will consider her poetry and prose in roughly chronological order.

All of her verse, however, is out of print, including the one edition of her poems, a two-volume 1889 selection prepared by two of her sisters. The only widely known lines of her poetry are the last half dozen in the "Statue of Liberty sonnet" that is often reprinted in anthologies that stress the democratic tone of American literature. Consequently, given their inavailability, larger portions of the poems are offered in this introductory work than might be expected.

My thanks are due to Dr. Hyman B. Grinstein, of Yeshiva University, who first set me straight about my subject; and to Dean David Mirsky, of Stern College for Women, for his encouragement. I am deeply grateful to Dr. N. H. Kaganoff, librarian of the American Jewish Historical Society, for his patient help, and to the society itself for permission to use the photograph of Emma Lazarus as frontispiece, and the manuscript notebook of Emma Lazarus and to publish material from it. The Metropolitan Foundation for Jewish Culture and its director, Dr. Jerry Hochbaum, demonstrated their confidence in the value of the subject of this book by giving me a grant-in-aid, and I hereby express my appreciation. Susan Dobkin and Simeon Vogel, as well as Aviva Wilkov of the Mehlman Library, Tel Aviv University, ably assisted in the research. To my wife, as ever, my inexpressible gratitude, and to the rest of the family, the dedication.

DAN VOGEL

Jerusalem College for Women,
Jerusalem, Israel

Chronology

1849	Born July 22 in New York City to Moses and Esther Lazarus.
1863	September 3, first dated poem: "In Memoriam: J.E.T."
1866–1867	*Poems and Translations, Written between the Ages of Fourteen and Sixteen.*
1868	Friendship with Ralph Waldo Emerson begins.
1871	*Admetus and Other Poems.*
1874	*Alide: An Episode in Goethe's Life* (novel). April 21, mother dies.
1876	*The Spagnoletto* (drama), privately printed.
1876–1881	Poems, translations, critical articles, reviews, and one story published in various journals.
1877	First translations made of medieval Hebrew poets (from German).
1881	*Poems and Ballads of Heinrich Heine* (translations). August, visit to Ward's Island refuge for Russian Jewish immigrants.
1882	*Songs of a Semite.*
1882–1883	"An Epistle to the Hebrews" (weekly essays).
1883	May-September, visit to England and France; December, "The New Colossus" ("Statue of Liberty poem").
1885	March 9, father dies. May-August, visit to England, France, Holland, Italy.
1887	*By Waters of Babylon* ("*Little poems in prose*"). Dies November 19 in New York City.
1889	*The Poems of Emma Lazarus*, two-volume selection by sisters.

CHAPTER 1

Poet and Prophetess

I New York and Its Jewry

THE family of Emma Lazarus's father was probably "Sephardic" (from the Hebrew name for Spain), a family of the Jewish community that lived in Spain and Portugal for centuries until 1492. The Inquisition sundered and then exiled the community into streams going eastward to Italy, Turkey, and Palestine, northward to Holland, and westward to the New World, to Brazil. Ultimately, twenty-three of those who ventured into the New World found themselves knocking on Peter Stuyvesant's door in New Amsterdam in 1654. They were not welcomed. Nonetheless, after some sharp words from Amsterdam, Stuyvesant reluctantly permitted them to stay. The great Jewish adventure in America had begun.

These Jews, and relatives who shortly followed, became merchants and respected members of a mercantile city. The coming of the British left them unaffected, but, remembering their own centuries of persecution, they rallied behind the revolution of 1776. They became the elite of American Jewry for the next 250 years. They considered themselves descendants of poets and philosophers of the medieval Golden Age of Hebraism in Iberia. So when the next wave of Jewish immigration came to New York from Middle Europe in the early nineteenth century, the "Ashkenazim" (from the Hebrew name for Germany) were considered beneath them. However, by the time Emma Lazarus was born, in 1849, the Portuguese Jews had absorbed the Germans and forced them upward into what one historian called the "higher stratum of Jewish society in New York. . . . In the 1830s, '40s, and '50s, they constituted an exclusive coterie whose members mingled only among themselves and married within their own group." [1] From one of these German families came Emma's mother, Esther Nathan. When she married Moses Lazarus, no one any longer looked askance at an Ashkenazi-Sephardi union.

When Emma Lazarus was born on July 22, 1849, New York had a population of about 330,000. Mingling in this population were 10,000 Jews. Although xenophobia characterized New York's melting pot, there was no overt anti-Semitism either then or during her lifetime, during which the Jewish community increased sevenfold. Unlike what happened during public troubles in Europe, not even during the Civil War draft riots in 1863 were the Jews molested. In New York, in those years, the Irish were the victims.[2]

Growing up Jewish was only as difficult as political and social emancipation made it. That is to say, Emma grew up, but not very Jewish. A later associate recalled that "the religious side of Judaism had little interest for Miss Lazarus, or for any member of her family." [3] In this regard, the Lazarus family followed the trend of old Spanish-Portuguese Jewish families that early began the drift into an assimilation into the American background. For thirty years, Jewish history was to be remote from Emma Lazarus, as far as her poetry was concerned.

II *Child of Her Class*

Emma was the fourth of seven surviving children of Moses and Esther Lazarus. Her poetic talent is perhaps an inheritance from her grandfather Eleazar Samuel Lazarus, a noted liturgist of his time who edited the standard liturgy for the Sephardic Shearith Israel Congregation, the first synagogue in New York.[4] (The congregation is still famous by its more popular name, "The Spanish-Portuguese Synagogue.") An uncle, Reverend J. J. Lyons, for whom Emma was to write a lovely eulogy in 1877, later became *hazzan* (cantor-minister) of the congregation.

Her father was a well-to-do sugar merchant before the Civil War and a wealthy one after it, but not by reason of illegal activities. He joined thousands of other businessmen who made fortunes out of the war by sheer shrewdness and volume. His house was one of culture and liberalism, as befitted a member of the old Jewish aristocracy of New York. His family lived in a fashionable area of the city and enjoyed summers in Newport, Rhode Island, where existed a little Jewish enclave surrounded by Protestant American stock. In later years, Emma herself said that she was "brought up exclusively under American institutions, amid liberal influences, in a society where all differences of race and faith were fused in a refined cosmopolitanism." [5] Supporting this statement is her sister Josephine's testimony that she was "without any positive or effective religious training." [6] This is probably too strong a statement. The family did observe some form of Sabbath and holy days, to which Emma will refer in later years, and they certainly attended services on Rosh Hashana (New Year) and Yom Kippur (Day of Atonement), experiences reflected in her later poems. Throughout her life her debt to the Old Testament is evident.

Undoubtedly her schooling was private. The only reference we have to the possibility of her having attended a school is her sister Josephine's passing reference to the poem "In Memoriam" (1867) as an elegy to "a school friend and companion." (*Poems*, I, 2) This remark probably means school-*age* friend and companion. As in most upper-class families of both Jewish and Christian communities, her parents engaged private teachers for her and her sisters.

From her first two books of poetry, published in 1867 and 1871, we can deduce what her education consisted of besides the "3 R's," geography, and so forth. Reading of European masters in their original languages and browsing in selected American poets constituted the staple of her enrichment. She learned German, French, and Italian in her teens well enough to publish competent translations. Authors she was to translate included Victor Hugo, Heinrich Heine, Goethe, Leopardi, and Petrarch. Later, her knowledge of German would introduce her to translations from the Hebrew of medieval Jewish poets of Spain, which she in turn translated into English. Her friend Rosa Hawthorne Lathrop (Nathaniel Hawthorne's daughter) said she knew Latin and Greek,[7] but we have no translations to prove it. Her course of study included mythology and legendry, a future source for poetic narratives. She studied music, which in time became an important inspiration for several cycles of poems as well as the basis for reviews of musical performances. Art seems to have become an interest at a later date in her life.

British poets of the sentimental Romantic school attracted her— Byron especially, and Shelley, Keats, Tennyson, and the Wordsworth of "Ode on Intimations. . . ." Indeed, even Shakespeare was to her chiefly a poet of the transiency of time and beauty. In American literature, Emerson and Longfellow headed the standard list of the New England poets, which included William Cullen Bryant. On the sly she surely read Edgar Allan Poe, who offered vicarious, delicious death, not uplift, to the impressionable teenager. With less need for caution, she probably read Hawthorne's stories and, in 1868 or thereabouts, his *American Notebooks* in Mrs.

Hawthorne's bowderlized version. These writers, together with Hugo and Heine, gave her a heavy dose of sentimentalism in literary art, idealized love and death in exotic settings, a tone of melancholy, and an atmosphere of darkness. According to Josephine, all this comported well with an innate personality that was somber, gloomy, even at times morbid (*Poems*, I, 3).

Above them all towered Ralph Waldo Emerson, who through his writings and presently by direct tutelage, urged her to see nature not in the wisps of time by moonlight, but as a sun-drenched organism of life, beauty, and imagery. She tried to shake off, but never really could, early melancholic tendencies. Yet, because of Emerson's admonitions, she came to read Thoreau and Whitman and professed a liking for them.[8]

There is little in Lazarus's output until 1880 that demonstrates an awareness of the upheavals occurring in American life. A few sentimental poems represent her entire reaction to the Civil War and the assassination of Lincoln. Of the sudden lurch toward industrialization and urbanization after the war there are similar inconsequential responses. Lazarus's concept of the poet, as we shall see, placed him above the earthly world, in a world of dreams. After 1880, she would modify this stance and show more interest in the actual world around her.

III *"Distinctly Feminine"—But Forward*

By 1877, Emma had published four books—poems, translations of poetry, and a novel—and was pursuing a busy and successful career as a lady magazine poet, with more critical acclaim than others in the profession. In New York, whether she liked it or not, she became famous and popular in the Jewish community. Jewish communal magazines reprinted her poems and her name was trotted forth as an example of a modern American-Jewish artist.

According to one biographical opinion, her mother's death in 1874 thrust Emma into herself and into a deep emotional dependence on her father.[9] The same sort of attachment affected Lazarus's contemporary, Emily Dickinson. And Emma, it is thought, like Dickinson, once loved and lost. He was Washington Nathan, a cousin on Emma's mother's side. Extant possible hints of her affection are a dedication of a poem to him and a possibly autobiographical cycle of poems ("Epochs," 1871) about a girl who suffered an emotional trauma. If it ever existed, the relationship came to nothing: the young man was accused of parricide, surely rare among Jewry, found not guilty, and faded out of the record of Emma's life entirely. She remained unmarried, like two of her sisters, but the fact never kept her from writing about love.

The dominance of Moses Lazarus, the vacuum left by her mother's death, and the lack of a romantic attachment certainly could lead to extreme shyness and overintrospection, and Emma is characterized as having these traits in abundance. Yet one of the most fascinating peculiarities about Emma Lazarus is the difference between what people said her nature was and what her public actions revealed. For example, Josephine Lazarus said of her sister's attitude to her work: "Once finished . . . her writings apparently ceased to interest her. . . . The public verdict as to their excellence could not reassure or satisfy her. . . . A true woman, too distinctly feminine to wish to be exceptional— . . . [there was] something more than modesty in her unwillingness to assert herself or claim any prerogative, something even morbid and exaggerated" (*Poems*, I, 8–9). The problem is that this characterization does not seem to accord with recorded facts.

This apparently shy, modest teen-ager sent her first book of poems to Ralph Waldo Emerson, no less! And Emerson responded, launching a rocky relationship that was to last for several years (discussed more fully in chapter 3). In her second volume, *Admetus and Other Poems* (1871), she dedicated a poem to Emerson. But a few years later, after Emerson left her out of his anthology *Parnassus* (1874), she wrote him a scathing letter of disappointment. This, it would seem, is neither indifference nor lack of self-assertion on Emma's part.

Admetus attracted the attention of Thomas Wentworth Higginson (1823–1911), the kindly *Atlantic* writer, who seems to have specialized in spinster poets. He was already involved with Emily Dickinson. Unlike the poetry of the recluse of Amherst, Emma Lazarus's poetry was straightforward and traditional. He heaped profuse praise on it. By 1876, their preceptor-pupil relationship ripened to the point where he rivaled Emerson as her personal critic.

Only to Emerson and Higginson did she entrust the reading of her play, *The Spagnoletto*. Higginson was less critical than Emerson. Lazarus's letter to Higginson of November 4 of that year notes, "I was . . . as much surprised as delighted with your cordial praise. . . . I do not know which to thank you most for—the careful, critical reading which you have been good enough to devote to my play . . . or your friendliness & sympathy in troubling yourself to give me the kind of criticism which you value most yourself, & indicating points that struck you most favorably." [10] As with Emily Dickinson, however, Higginson's critical attitudes had no essential effect upon Lazarus.

Shyness and modesty did not prevent Lazarus from a long correspondence with another popular American author of the time, the naturalist John Burroughs. Again, from the evidence in extant letters, it probably was Emma who started the correspondence. Burroughs replied on April 29, 1878: "I spoke of you to [Walt Whitman]. He remembered your name and had read & remarked some of your poems. They had arrested his attention, which you may consider a compliment." [11] They discussed Whitman's poetry and *Democratic Vistas* in their letters; Burroughs, with a touch of misogyny, was surprised that a woman enjoyed the *Vistas*.[12] By 1885, they were discussing two British Hebraists—Matthew Arnold and Thomas Carlyle—thus reflecting Lazarus's recent plunge into Jewish affairs. Her analysis of Jewish history, which found its way into poems and essays, troubled Burroughs, who urged her to adopt "a large & charitable view . . . & not insist upon the near-sighted personal, woman's view." [13] Burroughs's interlocutor does not sound in this correspondence like a male-dominated, retiring personality. And Lazarus's public and private utterances did not prevent Burroughs from writing a strong eulogy for her, in which he commented, "I think some of her poems rank with the best that have been produced in this country during her time." [14]

Her forwardness extended to foreign authors, too. To Ivan Turgenev she sent *Alide* (1874), her novel about young Goethe, and he replied with a note of rapture. When she went abroad in 1883, she was warmly received by Browning and Morris, to whom her work was known. Her list of admirers includes Charles Dudley Warner, John Greenleaf Whittier, Henry George, Charles Henry Dana, Henry James, William James, James Russell Lowell—a rather illustrious group for a presumably shy young woman who cared little for her public posture.

Yet another preceptor, E. C. Stedman, author and influential critic, made his appearance in the late 1870s. Some have credited him with turning Lazarus's interest to her Jewish heritage. But his prestige only gave authorization to a tendency already quietly evident. His relationship with Lazarus epitomizes the problem of determining to what extent her preceptors really affected her as an artist. Emerson demanded what she could not give, but no doubt opened her world of poetry a bit more. Burroughs made no headway in transforming her womanly heart. Higginson and Stedman merely solidified what was happening anyway. Emma Lazarus was of an independent mind. The influences upon her were all in the printed pages of literature; live ones she resisted with a dedicated self-confidence.

IV   *"Redoubtable Lady"*

We shall have occasion in the later chapters of this book to investigate more fully Emma Lazarus's transfer of allegiance from Olympus to Sinai, from general culture to Jewish history. Here it will suffice to comment on the events that broke into her comfortable world and formed the background of the radical change in her attitudes and interests.

In 1877, she admitted to an "ignorance that has given me heretical opinions in regard to Jewish genius," but she expressed herself "grateful to be taught the truth."[15] She did not appear quite so un-Jewish or ignorant to others, however. Ellen Emerson, in a letter of 1876, described Emma as "a real unconverted Jew (who had no objections to calling herself one, and talked freely about 'our church' and 'we Jews'), and to hear how the Old Testament sounds to her, and find she was brought up to keep the Law, and the Feast of the Passover, and the day of Atonement. The interior view was more interesting than I could have imagined. She says her family are outlawed now, they no longer keep the Law, but Christian institutions don't interest her either."[16] By the end of her life, remarks E. C. Stedman, though she displayed a broad intellectual attitude that had nothing of the isolation often attributed to followers of Moses' Law, he would not have been surprised had she returned to "Pentateuchal faith."[17] She never did, but clearly she was not in the 1880s the same woman who had written "Admetus" and other narratives inspired by Gentile cultures.

Hers was not a religious conversion but an historical and cultural one. The assassination of Czar Alexander II on March 13, 1881, served as the prelude to anti-Jewish pogroms in Germany and Russia. Newspaper accounts reported the horror of the events with long, lurid accounts, but their meaning did not immediately penetrate Emma Lazarus's secure New York Jewish circle, or the consciousness of Lazarus herself. This denseness was exemplified by the *Jewish Messenger*, the "organ of the Jewish upper class" that had discovered Emma Lazarus years before as a Jewish voice. As late as the early months of 1881, the *Messenger* editorialized against a liberalized

immigration policy. "The leading elements [of the community],"
writes Mark Wischnitzer, "belonged to the Americanized German-
Jewish immigrants [Lazarus's class], and they were slow or even loath
to organize relief in a measure worthy of such a community as
American Jewry represented at that time," because they had "insuffi-
cient insight into [the Russian victims'] mentality, their habits, cus-
toms and mode of life." [18] It was an attitude that Lazarus, child of her
class, never entirely lost, but she, together with her elite Jewish
contemporaries, did change predilections. The change was signaled
in the *Messenger*'s call for contributions to the Russian Relief Fund in
August 1881.

By coincidence, in that very month Lazarus visited Ward's Island
in the company of Rabbi Gustav Gottheil, and her whole world was
transformed. "The effect," writes Gottheil's biographer, "was
magical."[19]

Rabbi Gottheil had prophetically been instrumental in preparing
Emma Lazarus for this incandescent moment. He had four years
earlier introduced her to the world of medieval Hebrew poetry (see
chapter 10), which in turn led her to read about the history of Jewish
persecution in and expulsion from Spain. Long before, in an early
poem clearly influenced by Longfellow, she had agreed that the Jews
were a nation of the past. However, the migration of 40,000 Jews to
New York in two years filled her with an inspirational mixture of
indignation against their persecutors, horror at the squalor into which
they were forced on Ward's Island, and recognition of their essential
persistence and vitality. This was no dead nation.

She responded in two areas—writing and social action. Through
the printed word she tried to set right a whole tradition of misconcep-
tion about Jews, past and present. In the early 1880s she wrote a
series of polemic essays in which she defended the Jewish people
against their detractors, investigated the history of Christendom's
inhumanity toward the Jews, and inspected the Jewish character and
found it no worse than that of any other group. She raised a mighty
call for the Return to Zion, to Palestine, as the best solution for all
Jews (except those in America!). Strewn throughout this score of
essays is the evidence that Lazarus hungrily read a vast number of
books and articles about Jews written by Jews and Gentiles. We
might wonder whether she ever privately felt that her earlier education had been deprived.

Now came poems dealing with the same subjects, poems that
suddenly owed their existence to no published source, no Romantic

visionaries, no purveyors of melancholy. These poems came from an inner rage. They are filled with wrath, indignation, accusation, and pride in the Jew. It is these poems that invited the favorable comment of critics from Whittier in her own day to Van Wyck Brooks a half century later. *Songs of a Semite* (1882), which collected previously printed poems, a play on the subject of a pogrom in Germany in the fourteenth century, and translations of medieval Spanish Jewish poets made her unique among the lady poets of her time.

The social action she undertook was heralded in one of a series of essays published in November 1882 under the overall title of *Epistle to the Hebrews*. She wrote, "Antipathy to manual labor is one of the great social diseases of our age and country. . . . What we need . . . is the building of our national physical force." She even quoted the Talmud, the vast body of Jewish law and lore: "The Talmud says: 'Get your living shining carcasses in the street if you cannot otherwise; and do not say, I am a priest, I am a great man, this work would not fit my dignity.' " [20] This, from a privileged New York spinster, anticipates later exhortations on the same subject by essayists of political Zionism that inspired thousands to go to Palestine to retrieve the land and eventually to pioneer the rise of the State of Israel.

She trumpeted the call to manual labor as the way to save the dignity of the refugees in New York and to provide them with the means of earning a livelihood. In a letter to the *American Hebrew* in October 1882 discussing Jacob Schiff's refuge for the unfortunate Jews on Ward's Island, Lazarus quoted Herbert Spencer and Charles Darwin on the dangers of "ignorant . . . short-sighted philanthropy" and demanded the institution of technical and industrial education. There was a quick response to her "excellent programme":[21] a canning factory not far from the island hired all the women and older children in the refuge and transported them to and from work by boat. This is one of the incidents that have convinced recent writers on Emma Lazarus that she had Socialistic tendencies.[22] Certainly her reading of Henry George's *Progress and Poverty* in 1881 had something to do with this project; and in 1883 she was to visit William Morris's Socialistic factory in England. Yet, in the absence of anything political in her writings, her "Socialism" is not definitely much more than the term these critics have given to her activated humanism.

Lazarus was not satisfied with merely writing about these matters. She undertook communal action to further the cause. In 1884, she

became a driving force in the organization of one of the most successful projects of helping newly arrived victims of persecution—the
Hebrew Technical Institute. That she was a gadfly to realize this
dream is clear from the contemporary record. Richard Gottheil reports that Lazarus used his father, the rabbi, to arrange for a series of
meetings out of which came the founding of the School, and the
American Hebrew credits her with sowing the seeds of the idea.[23]

All this meant that this lady poet—shy, modest, and unassuming,
according to those who knew her—had to leave the sanctity of her
home, leave the walls that protected her virginal isolation, leap the
distance that separates a page of print from life, and plunge into the
masculine world of finance, proletariat training, building construc-
tion, face-to-face cajoling, arguing, convincing. But as we have
already suspected, the change was not so startling. She always had a
progressive notion of what a woman can and ought to do.

Indeed, Emma Lazarus has been looked upon as an early women's
liberationist. She had no program and no organization, not even a
philosophy of women's liberation. But she did have the inner
strength and pride that responded to the call of a social cause. That
this personal involvement violated the rules of feminine behavior in
her social class we may be sure is true. That it fulfilled as well a newly
revived vision of women in Jewish history we may accept as one of the
sources of strength to rebel against her Victorian upbringing. That it
also fulfilled her own self is, of course, obvious. As early as 1895 one
social historian recognized her contribution in these words:

While the movement for women's complete emancipation had counted not a
single Jewess among its promoters, its more legitimate successors, the movement to establish women's right and ability to earn a livelihood in any branch
of human endeavor . . . was headed and zealously supported by Jewesses,
[including] Emma Lazarus in America.[24]

At the height of her popularity and influence, Emma Lazarus
realized a dream—she sailed to visit England. She left on May 15,
1883. In England she met a galaxy of famous people—including
Robert Browning.[25] The meeting must have been an interesting one,
because more than ten years earlier Lazarus's version of the "Admetus-Alcestis" myth was being compared most favorably with Browning's own in his "Balaustion's Adventures" (see chapter 4). Lazarus
and Browning discussed his late wife's knowledge of Hebraism, and
this, too, had an undercurrent of more than formal courtesy. Emma
Lazarus was being classed in popular criticism with Elizabeth Barrett

Browning as a poet. From Browning's letter on June 24, 1883, we note happily that all went off amicably: he referred to her as "the redoubtable Lady, [a] vigorous [and] militant defen[der] of the Laws."[26]

Her visit with William Morris went extremely well. Not a word in the correspondence or in Lazarus's report on the visit in *Century Magazine* (published in July 1886) mentioned her published statement at the end of "Admetus" in 1871 that she did not plagiarize Morris's version of that legend (see chapter 8).

She was home by the end of September, soon plunging into writing new poems—of which one group, "By the Waters of Babylon," constituted experimental "little poems in prose" on the subject of the Jewish diaspora. Another was the sonnet "The New Colossus." The latter is by far her most famous piece of writing. Written for the Bartholdi Statue Pedestal Campaign for erecting the base of the Statue of Liberty in New York Harbor, the sonnet's last few lines are the well-known invitation to the persecuted and harassed that is embossed on the pedestal. Millions saw the words on their way to a new life on these shores.

V *"Winged Flight to Heaven"*

The spring of 1884 proved to be an active time. Lazarus wrote a second essay on Heine, in which she emphasized a theme she underplayed in the introduction to her book of translations three years before: the theme of Heine's Jewishness that burst out of his Lutheran veneer. She wrote a last tribute to Emerson upon his death, a sonnet that lauded him, but with reservations. In August, the first signs of her lethal illness appeared, and the peak of creativity passed.

On March 9, 1885, her father, Moses Lazarus, passed away. "The blow was a crushing one for Emma," writes sister Josephine. "Truly, the silver cord was loosed, and the golden bowl was broken. Life lost its meaning and its charm" (*Poems*, I, 32). She sailed again for Europe, this time not on a triumphant tour but in search of health. She stayed for two years, traveling to Holland, France, and Italy. Only two poems were written during this interval of time. Gravely ill with cancer, she returned on July 31, 1887.

On November 19, 1887, a Saturday, she died. She was buried on November 21, "in accordance with Jewish rites," [27] alongside her parents and ancestors in the burial plot for members of Shearith Israel Synagogue, in Cypress Hills Cemetery, Queens, N.Y. Obituaries

and notices appeared in all the New York newspapers. She was
thirty-eight years old.

VI *Afterglow*

The name of Emma Lazarus, however, did not yet die. The publications that had printed her poems and essays did not content themselves with mere formal notices of her death. On November 26 the
Critic wrote of her, "Miss Lazarus was a writer of originality and
force, both in verse and prose, and her death is a distinct loss to
American letters" (p. 279). On December 9, 1887, the *American
Hebrew* published a special memorial issue. Columns and columns of
tributes were printed, an international compendium of sorrow.
Emma Lazarus was referred to as a "Deborah" of her people, an
allusion to the great woman in the Book of Judges who led the
Israelites to victory over their enemy. Whittier said, "With no lack of
rhythmic sweetness, she has often the rugged sweetness, and verbal
audacity of Browning," and he called her the "sweet singing Miriam,"
(p. 3), referring to the incident in the Book of Exodus when Moses'
sister led the women of Israel in song after the parting of the Red Sea.
Henrietta Szold, the founder of the Hadassah Organization of America, paid tribute to her, not only as a woman poet, but as a woman
activist: "Her life held out a golden promise of that future when the
old Jewish spirit—women of culture and refinement not disdaining to
foster it tenderly—shall once more flame up with all the brilliancy of
the Spanish period she so devotedly studied" (p. 5).

Particularly appropriate tributes followed for months in the form of
sonnets in memoriam, bouquets of acknowledgment that a master
sonneteer had passed on. Charles de Kay, a friend and minor poet,
published "To Emma Lazarus" in the *Critic* for December 10, 1887,
tracing her early devotion to Hellas, and ending with calling her
"Sibyl Judaica" (p. 293). In February 1888, the editor of the *Century*,
Richard Watson Gilder, printed in his magazine—where Lazarus had
published her most fervent essays—a sonnet he had written on
November 19, the day she died. "Dear poet-comrade," he called her,
"thou of the old race/ That with Jehovah parleyed, face to face" (p.
581). Gilder wrote another memorial sonnet in 1905, in which he
referred to Lazarus as the "bard of the ancient people,/ Though being
dead, thou speakest. . . ." [28] Another admirer, Mary McKinney
McNeal, several months after Lazarus's death contributed a sonnet to
the *American Hebrew*, again bestowing upon her the appellation

"Sweet Miriam", and it was Mrs. McNeal who dubbed her "Poet and Prophetess" in this poem (April 6, 1888, p. 131).

A year after the death of the poet, the *Century* published a memorial number dedicated to her (October 1888), with its frontispiece the picture that has since become the most widely reprinted portrait. The picture impressed the aged Walt Whitman, who years before had discussed Lazarus with John Burroughs, but now apparently did not remember. "I know little about her work," he said to Horace Traubel (October 9, 1888), "but her face is an argument—a beautiful face." Next day Traubel reports:

W. had been reading some about Emma Lazarus today. "She must have had a great, sweet, unusual nature. I have meant to look more into her work, all I know of her has been casual—the things that come to here and there in the magazines and newspapers. I never met her—several times came near doing so. It may be gratuitous to say so—no doubt is—but I have randomly, wholly at random, believed she did not wish to meet me—rather avoided me. It may be gratuitous to say this, but I have had reasons for feeling its truth—good reasons, though reasons rather emotional than concrete. If she did deliberately set about not to see me she was put up to it." . . . Added as to Emma Lazarus: "She was as you say, quite different from the great body of professional women . . . [whose] purpose on earth [is] to be vitriolic, say bright things, provide a laugh." [29]

No evidence exists anywhere to support Whitman's curious suspicion. On the contrary, it represents a sad irony, for Lazarus had expressed to Emerson and Burroughs her admiration for his poetry.

In 1889, Houghton Mifflin published a two-volume *Poems of Emma Lazarus*. Selected by sisters Mary and Annie (Josephine's reprinted *Century* memoir served as the introduction), the edition is really a garland for deceased Emma, not an edited work.

One essay on her work appeared in the *Epoch*, April 1889, by Kate Upson Clarke, and a poem in the *Century* for February 1890 by Margaret Crosby. Clarke found Lazarus's poetry "chaste and pellucid," a good example for "passion-poets of today" to follow back "to clear forests of classic inspiration." Sadness and melancholy shadow her work, Clarke continues, and therefore it lacks "that gift of sensuous rhythm . . . that magnetic wildness of erratic phrase." [30] Crosby's sonnet says nothing new and is pedestrian besides, but it serves to show that Lazarus was not forgotten by the reading public two and a half years after her death.

In scholarly histories and estimates of American literature she was

noticed briefly but favorably [31] every fifteen years or so until 1939. In
that year, as a by-product of his great edition of Emerson's letters,
Ralph L. Rusk published his slim collection of letters to Emma
Lazarus in the Columbia University Library. In a little encomium in
the preface, he called her "laureate of the Jews," but one who "cared
much for freedom and social justice for all peoples." "She was a lesser
Whittier, with a special cause to sing." [32]

In 1944, Morris U. Schappes published a selection of poetry and
prose. Around the hundredth anniversary year of her birth, 1949,
appeared Morris U. Schappes's edition of her letters, a spate of
articles, mainly in Jewish magazines, and Arthur Zeiger's dissertation
(1951). Since then she has been largely forgotten.

CHAPTER 2

Poems and Translations
of a Sentimental Girl

A proud and indulgent father paid for the publication of Emma Lazarus's first book of poems. She was all of seven years of age when the world was confronted with *Poems and Translations by Emma Lazarus written between the ages of Fourteen and Sixteen*. Her debt is noted in the dedication, "To My Father, Dec. 12, 1865."[1] The contents are divided into three sections: "Original Pieces," about thirty-five poems, including a sixty-page romance, "Bertha"; "Translations from the German", fifteen short lyrics, all from Heinrich Heine; and "Translations from the French," comprising one song from Alexandre Dumas and twenty from Victor Hugo, whose name heads that subdivision.

Original or not, almost all these poems are of a piece: they are cast in the melancholy mode. Today, after the "New Criticism" has taught us that sophistication, impersonality, ambiguity, and symbolism are the criteria of great poetry, we may tend to sneer at the adolescent themes of malaise-of-life, the superficial emotions, and the tiresome poetic diction that characterize this volume. Yet a famous contemporary, William Cullen Bryant, thought these poems "better than any verses I remember to have seen written by any girl of eighteen."[2] No less a personage than Ralph Waldo Emerson regarded them so highly that he tried to make the poetess a disciple. Years later, William James remembered the pleasure he derived from reading "the simpler little things" in this first book of Emma Lazarus's poems.[3] These effusions of an as yet unformed talent cannot then be dismissed as mere juvenilia. We must seek the dormant qualities that lie beneath what one writer called "the conventionally romantic and vaguely melancholy themes congenial to youth."[4] We shall discover, alongside the bad habits of versifying that she never got rid of, flashes of independence of form, gracefulness of writing, and expression of perennial, uncomplicated emotions that in time endeared her to readers in all areas of American life.

I "Shadows of Evening"

In "The Echo," dated October 12, 1863, Emma Lazarus writes an unwitting characterization of her poetic self in these years:

> When the shadows of evening fell low on the earth,
> Then I climbed the steep side of the mount old
>   and bare,
> Whose dark, slender top seemed to cleave the
>   blue air,
> And then sadly I mused on the death of my love,
> Looking down upon forest, and meadow, and grove.
>
>   (*Poems and Translations,* 6)

Immaturity runs rampant. The elements of conventional themes and trite prosody in this poem very nearly make it an unconscious parody of her early practice. Yet it must be said that Lazarus was inspired to write this sort of thing not only by the natural predilections of youth toward imagined catastrophe, but by the tonal influences of popular poets on both sides of the Atlantic. It is not surprising that she would be influenced by poets still alive or only recently dead who commanded the admiration of her elders and betters. What is more surprising is the assimilative ability she displayed in fitting their manner to her own talents.

II *Echoes of Poe*

That the poetry of Edgar Allan Poe danced in Lazarus's adolescent consciousness in 1863–64 is probably true, although no direct evidence of her admiration is recorded until much later. It is an influence of manner, tone, and theme, mainly, but direct suggestions of images may also be noted. A few examples will testify to the nature and extent of this influence.

"The Echo" probably has an analogue in "The Raven." Lazarus's persona is a bereft lover, who, like the speaker of "The Raven," asks desperate questions about his lost beloved:

> "Where again can I see Her? Oh, tell me but where!
> But the merciless heaven my cry will not hear!"
> Then the love mountain-echo gave answer,—
>   "Not here."

> "Shall I e'er see again my youth's hope, my one love?
> Oh, now answer, ye heavens, that smile, so above!"
> And the lone mountain-echo gave answer,—
>   "Above!"
>
> *(Poems and Translations, 6, 7)*

"By that Heaven that bends above us," cried Poe's desperate persona, "Tell this soul . . . if within the distant Aidenn" Lenore can be found: but, "Quoth the Raven/Nevermore," a laconic refrain, like Lazarus's mountain echo. The raven does not ever vouchsafe any assurances to the bereaved, but Lazarus, with all the certainty and naiveté that a romantic teen-ager is capable of, pens a conclusion of faith and hope. The mountain echo assures the beloved he will one day see her "Above!"

A dead lover, a sepulcher, and sad memories drift over from Poe's "Ulalume" to Lazarus's two-stanza "Holy of Holies." In Stanza I, the lover dedicates a chapel to his "pure Madonna"—

> And I deemed that form of beauty
>   From my soul would ne'er depart,
> For the maiden was my idol,
>   And the altar was my heart
>
> *(Poems and Translations, 19)*

—before which he burned a taper in her honor. In Stanza II, however, death had sundered the love.

> I call the taper Mem'ry, now, . . .
> And I weep before my altar
> Now with prayerless lips apart,
> For my idol now is broken,
> Like my mocked and ruined heart.
>
> *(Poems and Translations, 19)*

One critic places at Poe's door all the dead beautiful women in Lazarus's *Poems and Translations*, because Poe said in "The Philosophy of Composition" that this is the most effective theme for poetry.[5] That essay was published in 1846. Where would Emma Lazarus have seen it twenty years later, and would she, at the age of fourteen, have been patient enough to read it? It is reasonable to assume that the young adolescent would be interested more in reading verse than in reading poetic theory. Beautiful ladies die in Lazarus's verse simply because death and beauty are sublime states to the teen-ager, and the attraction of Poe is thereby explained.

Once, at least, Lazarus reversed Poe. Her poem "The Sea Queen's Toilet" (dated April 20, 1864), it has been said, owes much to Poe's "Annabel Lee," because both have mystical sea imagery.[6] Annabel ends up in a sepulcher by the sea, but Lazarus's Sea Queen is very much alive, sporting about in a submarine never-never palace. Rather, the prosody of Poe's "Bells" is a more likely legacy here than the melancholy mystery of "Annabel Lee":

> Under the sea, far under the sea,
> In the depths of the glorious sea,
> Sets the Queen of the Mermaids, laughing and singing,
> The pearly drops out of her golden hair wringing,
> Weaving them all
> In a coronal
> For the King of the Ocean, her husband to be.
>
> *(Poems and Translations, 8)*

We note the repetition of phrase and rhyme, the intermixing of long and short lines, the staccato trimeter in the center of the stanza, and the long, sustained single sentence. It is not surprising that Poe's powerful prosody in "The Bells" would ring long in one's ears. Yvor Winters once said that Poe's art was calculated to delight the heart of a servant girl.[7] We see now that he succeeded with aristocratic adolescents, too.

III   *The Sorrows of Tennyson*

Another, even more obvious, influence came from the popular sentimental lyrics and romances of Alfred Lord Tennyson. Lazarus's very first poem, dated September 3, 1863, when she was but fourteen years old, is entitled "In Memoriam: J. E. T.," a blatant imitation of the title of Tennyson's "In Memoriam: A. H. H." Whoever "J. E. T." was, she could not, of course, inspire this teen-ager to the depths of sad wonder and doubt and the heights of poetic expression to which the death of Hallam carried Tennyson. That Lazarus imitates Tennyson even to this small extent indicates both her lofty aspiration and her sentimental taste. Her poem is full of languishing emotion about a girl who died in the flower of her youth:

> One by one the summer flowers
> Now are dying;
> She, the fairest of them all is
> With them lying.

Though J. E. T. was a contemporary, we do not get the feeling that Lazarus sees her as a counterpart of herself, as Milton saw Edward King in "Lycidas" or Shelley saw Keats in "Adonais," two poems Lazarus very likely knew. Lazarus is enjoying the imagined spectacle of beautiful death too much to feel it. This is merely an exercise in verse-writing on a ready-made theme.

Nevertheless, there is one connection between her pastoral elegy and theirs: Lazarus uses the "cycle of the seasons" metaphor. The dying summer flowers are presently finished off by "Wintry snow- . . . stern misfortune's nipping blast." Having reached this nadir of the cycle, Lazarus, like the other elegists, now turns to an upward struggle

> . . . The flowers that are now all
> Quickly dying,
> At the blast of Autumn's keen breath,
> Lowly lying,
> They will bloom in future spring-times,
> Bright as ever.

Indeed, in a conclusion of faithful resignation, Lazarus, like Shelley enshrining Keats as a star in heaven, envisions

> The soul of that fair maid of
> Early doom
> In the Spring of heaven above will
> Once more bloom.
>
> (*Poems and Translations*, 2–3)

Thus, in the earliest stage of her career, Lazarus wedded nature to melancholy. Only occasionally will she free the two from this embrace.

The example of Tennyson's romances sanctified Lazarus's imaginings of love and death in narratives set in exotic places and peopled by melodramatic characters enacting melodramatic events. Indeed, the *New York Times* reviewer of *Poems and Translations* chided Lazarus with kindly humor by including Tennyson among her translated poets! [8] Arthur Zeiger credits Byron with some influence at this stage,[9] but, while the presence of Byron cannot be denied, his romances have more action and passion than Lazarus was ready for.

The poet of *Idylls of the King* and "The Lady of Shallott" is faintly echoed in Lazarus's romance "Bertha," a story of sundered love in an elaborate dream-setting of castles and royalty in eleventh-century France. Bertha marries Robert, son of Hugh Capet, on a day when "the azure sky was flecked with snow-white clouds" (*Poems and Translations,* p. 63). Her innocence, beauty, and ecstasy are further symbolized by the happiness of flowers who witness the glances of the lovers "melt[ing] into tenderness and love." But as the couple are about to leave the chapel, "a dark gray cloud/ Passed o'er the sun," and the shadow of the high altar falls in the shape of a coffin—an instance, of course, of too-obvious symbolism. Bertha is startled, and is consoled by her bridegroom, "But he too trembled at the omen dread" (*Poems and Translations,* p. 68).

It comes to pass that the Pope discovers the bride and bridegroom are "blood allied" and declares the marriage void. Robert and Bertha refuse to part, however—Robert defying the Pope in a speech of tired love clichés, but Bertha in a speech of heady defiance:

> Let the Pope [she cries]
> . . . with his mighty power . . . first
> Unbind the surging Ocean's silver chains,
> That coil around him from the moon on high
> Or bid him part the rainbow from the air,
> Tear the gold bolt that dwells within its folds—
> Ere he essays to part two tender hearts.

This is bombast, yes, but the arching imagery is not at all bad for a sixteen- or seventeen-year-old.

When they are excommunicated, Bertha takes upon herself all the blame, refuses to accept her husband's disavowal of her responsibility, and swoons into a coma, during which she gives birth to a prince. End of Part I of "Bertha."

Part II reveals the rank Gothicism in Lazarus's Romanticism at this time. The action resumes in a monastery ruled by a cruel abbot, Helgant, who feels impelled to prove to the world that the reward of Bertha and Robert's sinful defiance cannot be the issuance of a beautiful prince. It so happens by coincidence that the monks had been caring for a deformed foundling, and a horrible plot forms in the abbot's twisted mind. First he kidnaps the tiny new-born prince and drowns him, as

> The happy birds sang their loving songs,
> The azure sky smiled down upon the Land.

Lazarus, it would seem, wants us to remember that she had used the same nature images in her description of Robert and Bertha's wedding day, and the reprise here is meant to convey the irony that this terrible act had been anticipated in the working of Fate.

The plot progresses. Helgant exchanges the "monster babe" for the drowned prince, commenting upon the visage of evil in the deformed child, a fitting gift for the incestuous couple. When Bertha espies this child at her side, she at first disbelieves the abbot's insistence that it is hers. But when the monks perjure themselves and swear it is, she accepts the child and asks Helgant to present him to King Robert. This scene occurs as—in another nature image—the stars outside ironically "twinkled forth/From out the azure mantle of the skies."

The poem ends with Bertha in a convent, parodying her earlier marriage ceremony in a wedding to the Christ. She is dressed in white and prostrates herself once more at the altar. The priest announces that she is dead, but the nuns take this figuratively to mean that her old sinful self has parted. However, in an ultimate thrust of heavy iron, "The chants were true, for she was *dead*" (*Poems and Translations*, p. 118; Lazarus's italics).

The passages quoted from this poem illustrate a side of Lazarus's talents that becomes more and more evident in her canon. The poem is about 1,300 lines of blank verse, and, for all the triteness of imagery and vision, displays a surprising sure-handedness in one so inexperienced. She uses enjambment with some skill. She keeps the meter, but not monotonously. She writes fast-moving narrative with fast-moving verse, and slows down the pace with vocabulary that is pentameter but pulls the reins. This response to freedom from conventions of rhyme she would hereafter display only occasionally, fearful of straying too far from the trodden path of tradition. But when she does, she will sound more modern and interesting than in most of her lyrics.

Suspense, foreshadowing of irony, and envelopment of Gothic mystery and terror maintain consistent narrative interest, but characterization is another matter. Unidimensional portrayals of the pure, suffering heroine; of the stalwart but weak hero; of the leering,

gloating villain—all of whom tear passions to tatters, pull the story
down to abject melodrama. And there it rests, as a tribute to Lord
Tennyson. We shall see the same dichotomy of storytelling abilities in
her later narratives, whether in the form of prose, poetry, or drama.

IV   *Tears from the Continent*

A long acquaintance with the poetry of Victor Hugo resulted in a
spurt of translation from April 2 to July 2, 1865. These ninety days saw
twenty dated translations and eight more poems without specific
dates. Who can conjecture what such an immersion into melancholy,
elegy, and cynical sentiment might have done to Emma Lazarus?
What effect would a poem like Hugo's "At Villequier" (translated
May 20, 1865), for example, have on an impressionable, sensitive
sixteen-year-old girl who aspires to write verse? The speaker of "At
Villequier" is a parent of a sixteen-year-old girl who has just died—
"this child we so tenderly love, / [who had made] the light of our
house, and day in our heart" (*Poems and Translations*, p. 144). God in
this poem is purported to be "Good and clement, indulgent and mild"
(*Poems and Translations*, p. 145), but makes man's life short and
solitary, never mirthful or joyous. "Man's an atom in all this infinite
gloom," caught up in "Creation [which is] only a great giant wheel"
(*Poems and Translations*, p. 148). Hugo's touch of ironic Naturalism,
of course, passed by Lazarus, for whom the idea of delicious death
(and of an exact contemporary at that!) and the simple, tearful sentimentality were quite sufficient.

Relating visions of death to themes of love is not difficult. Here,
too, Hugo solidifies the Romanticism of young Lazarus, as in the
translations "The Rose and the Butterfly" and its sequel "L'Envoi:
to—" (June 25, 1865). The rose and the butterfly "well . . . do love"
and they "resemble each other, 'tis said that we are/ Each one, a
bright flower" (*Poems and Translations*, p. 171). The rose complains,
however, that the butterfly can fly, whereas she is chained to the
ground. Nevertheless, she is ready to sacrifice for love:

> Oh, I would with my perfume embalm thy winged flight
>   To heaven's high gate
>   (*Poems and Translations*, 171)

But in "L'Envoi: to—," love leads to death eventually:

> All, roses and butterflies, together Death brings,
>   Come, oh wilt thou not live with me somewhere, my love?
>   For what dost thou wait?
>   (*Poems and Translations*, 173)

The indelicate proposition, in the same tradition as, if less witty than, Marlowe's "To His Coy Mistress," fell on innocent ears. For Emma, the union of love and death is all her passion.

Thus, in the undated "Lamp of the Ganges," she elaborates on a Hindu legend of love-*cum*-death (synopsized in the headnote) which tells of the custom where maids of the Ganges, after their lovers leave them for a while, sail lamps on the river; if the lamp stays lit then the absent lover is true; if, however, the lamp goes out, the lover is faithless. In Lazarus's version, one bereft girl sails her lamp on the river, watches it flicker and then catch. But her momentary happiness dies with the dying lamp, and the bereft girl drowns herself in the might river, which immediately recovers its smooth, implacable flow. Thus is symbolized the care-less cosmos.

The same themes of momentary, unrequited love and dateless death prevail in the fifteen songs she translated from Heinrich Heine, all of them in the Hugovian manner. A few titles indicate the subjects: "Fleeting Kisses," "The Rose, the Lily, the Sun, and the Dove," "That Thou Lovest Me." Further quotation would be superfluous. For the second printing of *Poems and Translations* Lazarus added a long poem called "Recollections of Shakespeare," inspired by Heine's essay on "Shakespeare's Women." [10] Lazarus's recollections are entirely a dream of Shakespeare's melancholy heroines, some of them unlikely candidates for this exercise. They are led by the tragic Juliet and include the sad Miranda, Ophelia "beautiful as love . . . floating downstream," Desdemona, Cordelia, and even Beatrice and Imogen, whose love was not smooth but not tragic, either. Yet who knows what goes on in a teen-age girl's mind? As Geraldine Rosenfeld remarked, Emma Lazarus liked the "expression of Heine's love-disappointment, his youthful pessimism, his romantic retreat into the 'realm of hallucination,'" [11] and transferred the mood to her own lyrics. One day Lazarus would devote to Heine an entire book of translations as the climax of her early devotion to his themes. She never knew to what extent he and Hugo contributed decadence to her Romanticism.

V   *Moments of Natural Joy*

Quite different are two remarkable poems dealing with nature written by Lazarus in 1865–66. No doubt they were inspired by the writings of Ralph Waldo Emerson rather than by European sentimentalists. The one entitled "Links" is perhaps the more astonishing. The entire poem consists of only six lines, and for a piece written as early in its author's career as April 6, 1865, it is a notable achievement:

LINKS

The little and the great are joined in one
By God's great force. The wondrous golden sun
Is linked onto the glow-worm's tiny spark;
The eagle soars to heaven in his flight;
And in the realms of space, all bathed in light,
Soar none except the eagle and the lark.

(Poems and Translations, 27)

Concise, controlled, implicative, devoid of poetic diction, the imagery here is not smothered by adjectives of melancholy or by funereal Gothic settings. The poem is as free as the birds in it. So natural is it in syntax, enjambment, and vocabulary that we must look again to note that it rhymes.

Refracting a wide vision into a small prism, the poem can actually stand explication, because its imagery is suggestive, not obvious and overbearing. It begins with an hypothesis, the Great Chain of Being, but the idea is immediately concretized in imagery. At the top of the chain is "God's great force," which cannot be imagized. Immediately below shines "the wondrous golden sun"; at the other end of the chain, the "glow-worm." Lazarus does not choose an ant or amoeba to represent the smallest animate particle, but the glow-worm, so that the relation of the smallest mortal being to the most grand and bright heavenly luminary can be discerned in the glow-worm's "tiny spark." Into the intervening void soars the eagle, the ravenous bird, who actually strikes for heaven. He is balanced by his companion, the lark, the bird of song and dawn, beauty and promise, as in her beloved Shakespeare's Sonnet 29. Thus poet and peace fly together in the firmament.

The absence of man in the poem is obvious; his place in Lazarus's scheme can only be conjectured. His symbol is the lark, for it is with the lark, the bird of hope, that man's spirit, as in Shakespeare's sonnet, will soar. Lacking wings, man must soar only in imagination, in poetry.

This is a poem after Ralph Waldo Emerson's heart and no doubt was one of the *Poems and Translations* that attracted its author to him as a possible disciple.

Her theme parallels his *Nature* of 1836 as to cosmological vision; indeed, it might even be considered a restatement by an unformed, young poetic mind of the little poem Emerson used as the "motto" for his essay of that name in 1849:

> A subtle chain of countless rings
> The next unto the farthest brings;
> The eye reads omens where it goes,
> And speaks all languages the rose;
> And striving to be man, the worm
> Mounts through all the spires of form.[12]

Lazarus shows herself to be, for the moment, at least, a poet of Nature who aspires to commune with God, who perceives the spiritual facts behind the natural facts, and who employs the language of natural imagery to express the impulses of an individual soul. In accordance with Emerson's preachment in his essay, Lazarus distills diversity into unity through the medium of the symbol taken from nature. Moreover, the diversity she reconciles is not a paradox, which Emerson abhors, of good and evil. The lark, the eagle, all nature is an emanation of "God's great force," testimony to the moral hierarchy of the universe, as Emerson had himself poetized it in "Each and All" (1839). It was worth all of Emerson's patience to suffer through the gushy poems to come across this microcosm of Transcendentalism. "Links" was the only poem of this first collection deemed worthy of inclusion in the *Poems* of 1889.

Five months after she wrote "Links," Lazarus was inspired by a visit to Niagara Falls to write another brief nature poem. Possibly she recalled Emerson's inclusion of Niagara among the natural objects that the poet "overhears . . . and endeavors to write down the notes without diluting or depraving them." [13] In this poem, she fashions a different order of symbolism from the one she used in "Links":

NIAGARA

> Thou art a great altar, where the Earth
> Must needs send up her thanks to Him above
> Who did create her. Nature cometh here
> To lay its offerings upon thy shrine.
> The morning and the evening shower down
> Bright jewels,—changeful opals, em'ralds fair.
> The burning noon sends floods of molten gold,
> The calm night crowns thee with its host of stars,
> The moon enfolds thee with her silver veil,
> And o'er thee e'er is arched the rainbow's span,—

The gorgeous marriage—ring of earth and Heaven.
While ever from the holy altar grave
Ascends the incense of the mist and spray,
That mounts to God with thy wild roar of praise.

                                    (*Poems and Translations*, 42)

The poem is a blank-verse sonnet, and a harbinger of many fine things that Emma Lazarus was to do in this genre. At once, in this early example, she displays independence in dallying with the quatrained structure and in ignoring rhyme schemes entirely. The blank verse permits unobtrusive irregularities that highlight the meter, and allows for normal syntax and enjambment. On the other hand, habits of poetic diction, inversions, and fashionable archaisms, do creep in.

The imagery is appropriately lofty for this magnificent wonder of the natural world. The majestic metaphor is that of a natural "giant altar" on which Nature herself makes offerings of thanksgiving for the creation of the Falls. The coloration of the spray at dawn and at dusk appears to the poet as jewels, at noon as gold, and at night, reflecting moon and stars, as diadem and veils—all gifts at the natural shrine. The culmination of the image system in this poem is the Falls as altar at which the marriage of earth and heaven takes place, the rainbow being the ring and the mist the incense.

In the working-out of the metaphor, Lazarus displays good poetic judgment. She is clever, but not arch. Her strategy brings us from a statement of the metaphor to a climax that ends on a note of near-ecstasy. For the last thrust of the imagery, the poet suddenly transfers our sensibilities from sight to sound, concluding on a transcendent hosanna—a "wild roar of praise"—reaching up to the Almighty Creator.

But Lazarus, in all truth, was not capable in 1866–67 of sustaining this level of poetry. The attraction of the trite-if-true was too much. In the sequel to "Niagara" that she wrote a few months later, "Niagara River Below the Falls" (dated November 3, 1865), she ingenuously and unwittingly pens a critique of her own poetry to this moment:

The rush, the roar, the agony are past;
The leap, the mighty fall, are o'er at last;
And now with drowsy ripplings dost thou flow,
All murmurings in whispers soft and low.

                                    (*Poems and Translations*, 43)

Too true. The roar of "Niagara," the leap of "Links," quickly fall to drowsy ripplings and murmurings of inversions and tired rhymes. But—if we may continue her metaphor for another line—in every river there are moments of white water, where desire and power rise above stationary rocks.

VI *Echoes of the Civil War*

That her country was locked in a fratricidal struggle in the years 1863–65, while she spent summers in Rhode Island writing poems, finds expression in only three poems among the collection published in 1866–67.[14] This circumstance is not too surprising. The war never touched her family, except to make her father's business prosper. They spent summers by the sea and were probably out of town when the New York City draft riots of July 1863 raged on their doorstep on 14th Street. On the other hand, given Emma's state of mind in these years, war might have offered a ready-made world of sorrow and ironic destiny in which to compose visions of pain and death and sweethearts left behind. For some reason, however, few of these possibilities commended themselves to her consciousness, and then only in the elegy she wrote for "Brevet Brigadier-General Fred. Winthrop. Killed at the Battle of Five Forks, April 1, 1865."

What connection, if any, General Winthrop had with young Emma Lazarus is unknown. More than likely she read of his death in a casualty list and chose him as an anonymous symbol of the War Dead. Beyond the title, the poem says nothing personal about the deceased. Indeed, except for the title, it sounds nearly exactly like any of her earlier elegies. Though in the first stanza she does mention "the bitter struggle" and "Victory," the allusions are so hazy that connection with the Civil War is tenuous. As usual, she moralizes that

> The shadow only we can see,
>   Through blinding mists of tears;
> God sees the dazzling light that will
>   Illumine future years.

> (*Poems and Translations*, 29)

Flowers with "early blossoms fair," "silver stars," and "birdlings fair" weep and bear his praises upward. But at the climax, characteristically,

> . . . the saddest of ye all
> Is she who *cannot* weep.

> (*Poems and Translations*, 30; poet's italics)

Lazarus does a great deal better in two poems occasioned by the assassination of Lincoln: "April 27th, 1865" (written on April 29) and "The Mother's Prayer." In both, Lazarus adopts a perverse point of view. The first poem imagines the assassin's feelings and thoughts during the two horrible weeks the Union Army searches for him; the other imagines what his mother feels. In view of the profound national mourning that surrounded her, these are extreme displays of youthful sentiment for the underdog. Indeed, Lincoln's funeral cortege passed near her home in New York City just two days before she cast her tearful lines for John Wilkes Booth.

Lazarus's poem closely follows the reported facts: Booth was hurt in his leap from Lincoln's box at Ford's Theatre, was hounded for ten days from place to place in his flight, and finally was caught in a barn that later his pursuers set afire. These events are indirectly alluded to as the poem progresses.

There are five stanzas, the first three are spoken by Booth, the last two by the poet. Each stanza is punctuated by a refrain that counterpoints the stanza. The flavor of the verse and point of view can be tasted in the first stanza. The fugitive has stopped at a farmhouse:

> "Oh, where can I lay now my aching head?"
> The weary-worn fugitive sadly said.
> "I have wandered in pain all the sleepless night,
> And I saw my pursuers' distant light
> As it glared o'er the river's waves of blue,
> And flashed forth again in each drop of dew.
> I've wandered all night in this deadly air,
> Till, sick'ning, I drop with pain and despair."

The farmer's reply becomes the poem's refrain:

> Go forth! Thou shalt have here no rest again,
> For thy brow is marked with the brand of Cain.

This chorus actually is the only direct comment that the assassin is a criminal worthy of condemnation. Everywhere else in the poem, Lazarus tries hard to engender pity for him, as in the second stanza where even the possibility of divine condemnation is mollified by sympathy for the killer's plight:

> "I am weary and faint and ill," said he,
> "And the stars look down so mercilessly!

> Do ye mock me with your glittering ray,
> And seek, like the garish sun, to betray?
> Oh, forbear, cruel stars, so bright and high;
> Ye are happy and pure in God's own sky.
> Oh, where can I lay me now down to sleep,
> To rest and to slumber, to pray and weep?"

The answer to this plea is again the refrain of the poem which brands him with the mark of Cain.

After another stanza in the same tone accompanied by its attendant chorus of rejection, the poet takes over the telling of the flight. Sympathy for the fugitive is increased now by the fact that Nature joins in the persecution of him: he is beleaguered by rain and dew "on his fated head," he is maliciously led by "the will-o'-the wisp" . . . "o'er the swamp in the darksome night." Now it is not merely the voice of a cruel host who intones the refrain, but "all Nature's voices cried out again":

> Go forth! Thou shalt have here no rest again,
> For thy brow is marked with the brand of Cain.

In the final stanza, the pursuers catch up to the fugitive:

> One desperate struggle, and all is past,—
> One desperate struggle, 'mid smoke and flame.

The end is reached but not without a lachrymose farewell from the young poet:

> A prayer ascends to high Heaven's gate
> For his soul, —O God, be it not too late!

And with her characteristic feel for the melodramatic and ironic, Lazarus concludes her poem with the refrain now changed to read:

> All sorrow has gone with life's fitful breath.
> Rest at last! For thy brow bears the seal of Death.
> (*Poems and Translations*, 31–33)

The last lines, to be truthful, are meaningless. Sorrow does not die with the dying; indeed, it is the one inevitable legacy of death. And death cannot remove the brand of Cain from his brow; he is forever a murderer. But no matter: the climax befits the poem's tone. A sort of reconciliation in death is achieved, and that, for Emma, is satisfactory.

To tell the tale of the flight, Lazarus chose the anapest, "running meter," as the basic metrical unit of the line, but she modified it in an interesting manner:

> ˘   /   ˘ ˘ /   ˘ ˘ ˘ /   ˘   /
> "Oh, where can I lay now my aching head?"
> ˘   /˘   ˘   /˘ ˘   /˘   /
> " The weary-worn fugitive sadly said.

The opening and closing feet of the line are iambs (˘/), one syllable less than an anapest. This creates a limping anapest, strikingly appropriate to a limping fugitive. Whether young Emma thought out the variation of meter as more suitable to the situation of the poem, or whether she instinctively felt it, we have here an effective combination of form and content.

The monologue is realistic, yet poetic, not colloquial. Lazarus's favorite "o'er" grates elsewhere, but here we do not mind it. The rhymes, though common, do not sound tired, because they are absorbed, as it were, into the meter and the story. The coalescence of emotion and imagery marks a certain talent in a poet so young. All in all, given the age of the poet and the taste of the time, "April 27th, 1865" is no mean achievement.

The poignancy of the sequel, "The Mother's Prayer," again in modified anapest, is based on two features: the natural poignancy of a mother's soliloquy after the death of her son, regardless of his life's record; and the circumstance that in Booth's case the burial place was secret. He was first interred under the stone floor of the Washington Arsenal (only later was he reinterred in a Baltimore cemetery),[15] and the poem correctly imagines that his mother is ignorant of that fact:

> Oh, tell me where rises that misshapen mound?
>   [she cries]
> I will pray and will weep on the cold, clayey
>   ground.
> I would give all the joy of my happiest years
> To go there and shed these my bitterest tears.

His grave is "flowerless" and bereft of even a mother's vigil. She is ready to brave the perils of gloom and of darkness to go to it—even more:

> Ay, more than the night, I will go in the *sun*
> When my anguish and grief are seen by each one!
> Oh, break not thus rudely life's holiest ties,
> Let the mother now know where the fated son lies.

The last stanza carries a rather fine climax and a touch of sad, but not bitter, irony. The mother declares that

> I would go to his victim's revered, honored tomb,
> And beg, of that merciful heart in the gloom,
> His pardon and pity—*he* would not refuse!

Such a heart as Lincoln's would have permitted the mother the knowledge of where her son lay. And she would hasten to the grave to "whisper . . . to my doomed son" the victim's forgiveness. Then

> Sweet flowers . . . over his grave would arise
> To show that *God* knows where the fated one lies.
>   (*Poems and Translations*, 34–35)

God's benignity, greater than that of her son's judges, will be symbolized in the flowers that will grow from the grave.

That Emma Lazarus owed much to Tennyson's "Rizpah" for "The Mother's Prayer," as Arthur Zieger has noted, is probable.[16] Obviously, however, Lazarus does not achieve the dramatic force of that monologue in which Tennyson's persona emerges as a specific, complex, realistic character. Nor is she able to create so dense an atmosphere that we feel sucked into it. Lazarus's mother-persona and the ambience of her monologue are vague and typified. Yet Lazarus does achieve a measure of success.

Compared with the treacly elegies of much of the rest of *Poems and Translations*, these two poems show deftness of handling a difficult meter, control of tone, and avoidance of poetic diction. Pity is engendered, but without the overweening posing that Lazarus often permits in her graveyard verse. By 1865, she had reached a measure of control of her talents.

VII Reactions

In its own day, *Poems and Translations* was received with a good deal more kindness than the pervading unoriginality of most of the pieces called for. A reviewer in the *New York Times* treated the book with sweet reasonableness, finding the poems "chiefly remarkable because one so young produced them. . . . It could not be expected that one so young could create anything strikingly original herself." [17] On the other hand, we may suppose, he did not find Emma Lazarus slavish to her influences, for then he would have ignored the book entirely, like so many other pretty books by lady versifiers. After all, why should the initial effusions of a teen-ager demand his attention when Bryant, Longfellow, Emerson, Lowell, Stoddard, and others of their rank were publishing at the same time, if, at first glance, he did not see through the fog to glimpse the intermittent flashes of sun?

Twenty years after the publication of *Poems and Translations*, Josephine Lazarus, in the memoir of her sister, expressed the most important point of evaluation of the book:

Crude and immature as these productions naturally were, and utterly condemned by the writer's later judgment, they are, nevertheless, highly interesting and characteristic giving, as they do, the keynote of much that afterwards unfolded itself in her life.

(Poems, I, 2–3)

It is true that the themes of melancholy, unhappy love, and comfortable death cloud a good deal of Emma Lazarus's poetry at least until the 1880s. As regards her condemnation of these early effusions, however, we have only Josephine's word; no extant record contains such a judgment by the poet herself. Actually, at the time she seemed rather confident of her work; she sent a copy of the book to Ralph Waldo Emerson.

And the great man actually replied—and not merely with a polite note of receipt, but with appreciation and happy encouragement. In a letter of February 24, 1868, he says that he found that "some of these [poems] in the book are too youthful, & some words and rhymes inadmissible." These faults he would shortly undertake to correct. He thought "Bertha" too tragic and painful, "which I think a fault." Yet it is "carefully finished & well-told," and he would not be surprised if she were to send him "a heart-breaking tale [in defiance of his criticism] so rich in fancy, so noble in sentiment that I shall prefer it to all prosperities of time." [18] (She would soon try in *Admetus* in 1871.)

His overall estimate, substantiated by the poems she sent him soon afterwards, was—

The poems have important merit, & I observe that my poet gains in skill as the poems multiply, & she may at last confidently say, I have mastered the obstructions, I have learned the rules: henceforth, I command the instrument, & now, every new thought & new emotion shall [be made] eloquent to my own & every gentle ear.[19]

Thus began a master-disciple relationship that lasted for ten years.

CHAPTER 3

Emma and the Brahmin

IN one of those fortuitous coincidences of needs which literary history sometimes records, Emma Lazarus and Ralph Waldo Emerson came together—she the eager, young poetess with an actual book already published, he the Sage of Concord, the revered fountainhead of wisdom and poetry—in his sixty-fifth year.

Spiritually, her sister recalls, Emma at this age was "without compass or guide, without positive or effective religious training," and the writings of Emerson provided her with "the great moral revelation of her life . . . a golden rule of thought and action." She was exhilarated and intoxicated, Josephine Lazarus says. "His books were bread and wine to her" (*Poems*, I, 7–8). Emerson became her savior, and she his acolyte.

On his part, at about the time he received a copy of *Poems and Translations* on February 24, 1868, Emerson needed a disciple. Margaret Fuller, his feminist pupil on the *Dial*, had been dead fifteen years; Walt Whitman, after the first flush of approval in 1855, he now viewed distantly and darkly; Henry David Thoreau had died in 1862—the most deeply felt loss of all. Emerson looked for fresh talent to shape. May not the young authoress of "Links" and "Niagara" serve? For all her adolescent melancholy and Gothicism, she still drew on Nature for imagery. So, after a brief meeting at the home of mutual New York friends, in a letter of April 14, 1868, with serious whimsy, he appointed himself her professor and adviser.[1]

I   *The Poet, Books, and Nature*

The first lessons Emerson gave to Lazarus in his ensuing letters taught the role of the Poet. His advice sounds like restatement—sometimes revision—of passages in "The American Scholar" (1838) and "The Poet" (1841). Thus, glossing his famous epigram "Poets are liberating gods," he writes: "A true lover of poetry must fly wide for his game, & though the spirit of poetry is universal & is nearest, yet the successes of poets are scattered in all times & nations." [2]

Trying to break through Lazarus's provinciality and naiveté to liberate *her* spirit, Emerson seems to have reversed the order that he declared in "The American Scholar" was the educative process of a Poet. Instead of sending her first to Nature, he introduced her to books. "Books are a safe ground, but introductory only," he advises her. Though "books . . . tyrannize over our solitude" we owe gratitude to "our silent friends," because they offer "what I have never found & yet is admirable to me also." [3]

His suggestions for reading included Marcus Antoninus, Hippolyte Taine's essay on that philosopher, Wilkins's translation of the *Bhagavat Gita*, and Lesley's *Man's Origin and Destiny*. A strange First Reading List for a nineteen-year-old poetess!

Of course, Emerson preached to his disciple on the subject of Nature—the gateway, for him, to true experience, a knowledge of the spirit, and the language of poetry. "It is sufficient," he told her, "to have the eye opened to the miracle of Nature, & the ear to that music which reports it, & which we call poetry." [4] Characteristically, Lazarus's first response on this theme was to refer to her reading, not her experience. She reported to her teacher that she'd been reading Thoreau's *A Week on the Concord and Merrimack Rivers* and several poems by Walt Whitman. She gushed, "I no longer wonder at your admiration of Thoreau—what a noble, true, bold spirit his must have been—or rather is—for he is now more alive to me than many who are living near me." [5]

Actual sensuous experience finally entered her correspondence to the author of *Nature* when the early autumn of August 1868 inspired her to describe "with delight the thronging [?] trees of the woods, & the trembling poplars sprinkling their silver with gold, & the later flowers and fruits blooming and ripening." But she rushed on to say, "My tastes naturally lead me too much in the direction of retirement & isolation"—she feared contemplation of nature would turn her into "a permanent savage." [6]

She need not have worried. Emerson's dicta never transformed her into the kind of nature poet he idealized. And yet she was considered as one. For example, in her memoir Josephine Lazarus offers some lines from "Matins" written in 1871, as "picture after picture" of nature:

> To see the light
> That plays upon the grass, to feel (and sigh

With perfect pleasure) the mild breezes stir
Among garden roses red and white,
With whiffs of fragrancy.

(*Poems*, I, 10–11)

Sight, touch, and smell are all mentioned, but the picture is blurred
in a sort of synesthesia. Nevertheless, it is true that from natural
settings Lazarus received the initial imagery to write poems of what
Josephine termed "perpetual resource and consolation."

II *The Poet and His Times*

Having discussed books and nature, Emerson turned next to con-
temporariness. Here his admonitions to Emma Lazarus are an elaboration of the epigram in *Nature* that summed up his viewpoint: "The
invariable mark of wisdom is to see the miraculous in the common."
In a letter of January 20, 1869, he exhorts her:

Though you can throw yourself so heartily into the old world of Memory, the
high success must ever be to penetrate unto and show the celestial element in
the despised Present, & detect the deity that still challenges you under all the
gross & vulgar masks.[7]

She tried and did produce in 1869 a fine sonnet that combined both
nature and the commonplace:

LONG ISLAND SOUND
I see it as it looked one afternoon
In August,—by a fresh soft breeze o'erblown
The swiftness of the tide, the light thereon.
A far-off sail, white as a crescent moon.
The shining waters with pale currents strewn,
The quiet fishing-smacks, the Eastern cove,
The semi-circle of its dark, green grove.
The luminous grasses, the merry sun
In the grave sky; the sparkle far and wide
Laughter of unseen children, cheerful chirp
Of crickets, and low lisp of rippling tide
Light summer clouds fantastical as sleep
Changing unnoted while I gazed thereon
All these fair sounds and sights I made my own.

(*Poems*, I, 211–12)

She was absolutely right: for fourteen lines she handled sounds and sights with such precision and dexterity as to make them hers—and ours. There is no posed sentiment here, no trite moralism, no dulling of the sharp images. Moreover, though the structure of the sonnet is conventionally Petrarchan, the rhymes are not conventional: "o'er-blown/thereon," "strewn/sun," "chirp/sleep." The assonance and consonance are worthy of Emily Dickinson. For once, her versifying contributes to the discovery of the miraculous in the common.

And yet, performances like this are few. Lazarus's talent essentially lay in other poetic worlds, worlds which Emerson disliked. Sister Josephine was too extreme when she wrote that her sister "absorbed [Emerson's words] in her very being" (*Poems*, I, 8). The fact that Emerson eventually recognized Lazarus's innate resistance to what he thought was poetry colored the rest of their relationship.

III *Sheathed Words*

"I have noble friends," Emerson wrote to his young friend on October 28, 1868; "they send me high poetry—pictures of gods heroes & women bravely & adequately drawn." [8] He was referring to Lazarus's retelling of the Admetus-Alcestis myth. Thus began a short period in which Emerson directly criticized the text of several poems, some of which found their way into *Admetus and Other Poems* (1871); others had to wait until 1889 to be printed in her sisters' posthumous selection of her verse.

His critique of "Admetus" (extending over several letters) was typical of Emerson's method: always he began brightly and encouragingly about the poem, then suddenly he dampened his enthusiasm. "Admetus" had "fulness & high equality of power" but the speeches were "a line too long." [9] Revisions apparently did not help. When he reread the poem later, prior to offering it to the *Atlantic* on her behalf, he found some dialogue simply "not good enough," words, like "smileless," which were unacceptable, and wrenched metaphors: " 'Doubt' does not 'ravage' nor be 'revenged.' " Fifteen minutes with Shakespeare, he advised her, would show her how to prune weakness from dramatic passages. [10]

Emerson's critique of Lazarus's "Heroes" is most interesting because he not only offered criticism, but wrote suggested substitutions for certain lines. The poem is a paean to types of American heroes. It is dedicated to "the noble souls of half a million braves / [who lie]

Amid the murmurous pines"; to the martyrs of the Civil War "Who lie beneath the living beauty, dead,— / Beneath the sunshine, blind"; and to the living heroes who ply new kinds of heroism—hunting, harvesting on the western plains, plowing in New England, and "toiling in the town" (*Poems*, I, 55, 56, 57).[11]

Characteristically, the kindly critic began on a positive note: "The tone & sentiment of the poem are noble," and so effective that, when he read it to his wife, he reported, his voice faltered. Now came the "but" in his judgment. Because of the poem's excellence, it is worth improving the tenth stanza. He twitted Lazarus, "Did you ever read such a word as 'gainst' in Tennyson?" He felt that the stanza needed "stronger accent," the last line failing by reason of "absence of all force & melody." He added, "I have not at this moment time or facility to attempt a clean verse," but he offered the following anyway:

> The self-same men, with like audacious port,
> And with as stout endurance struggle on,—
> As sturdy, & as valiant in the street,
> As faced the blazing fort.[12]

Whether Emerson's version represents an improvement is moot—"stout endurance" is really no more fresh or powerful than Lazarus's original "dauntless purpose" or "defiant strength."

In any case, Lazarus's final version of the stanza is improved in diction, and the syntax, parallelism, and cadence flow with dignity and strength:

> Or, toiling in the town,
> Armed against hindrance, weariness, defeat,
> With dauntless purpose not to swerve or yield,
> And calm, defiant strength, they struggle on,
> As sturdy and as valiant in the street,
>   As in the camp and field.
>
> (*Poems*, I, 57–8)

IV *Parnassus Denied*

That Emerson was tiring of this extended tutelage was signaled on April 23, 1870, when he had to write: "I send back the Orpheus [another classical narrative published later in *Admetus*] with great humiliation" because other commitments precluded his reading it.[13] This was not the first time he had to delay his reading of a manuscript from Emma Lazarus, but it was the first time he returned one unread.

Though after several months' demurral, he accepted her dedication of the long poem "Admetus" to him in a letter of January 27, 1871,[14] this was the last substantive communication between them for three years.

Then the tempest over *Parnassus* broke.

Under that title, Emerson edited an anthology of English and American poetry by past and present poets chosen on purely subjective grounds. Time has not agreed by any means with all of Emerson's choices, but in any event Emma Lazarus was not among them. In truth, Emma had good reason for disappointment. *Parnassus* included about 450 poems, grouped under such headings congenial to Emma Lazarus's brand of poetry as "Nature: Land—Sea—Sky"; "Contemplative—Moral—Religious: Man . . . Fate . . . Sleep . . . Dreams . . . Death . . ."; "Dirges and Pathetic Poems." Of the 127 poets represented, from Geoffrey Chaucer to Henry Wadsworth Longfellow, many were great, many were immortal, many were famous. But Emerson also admitted to *Parnassus* selections from the works of a Mrs. Alexander (otherwise unidentified), Anna Laetitia Barbauld (*"Born in Leicestershire, Eng., 1743; died 1825"*), Sara H. (E. Foxton) Palfrey (*"Born in America"*), and other such worthies. He could find no space, however, for Emma Lazarus, not for a sonnet, not even for the six-line "Links." It is no wonder that the young, self-confident poet, led by the very editor of the anthology along the parnassian path, would feel shocked and ill-used.

On December 27, 1874, she sent off an angry letter of disappointment and betrayal. In it she quoted from his "flattering opinions & letters" (no doubt feeling that quoting from his adverse comments was inappropriate at this time). She asked with white-lipped courtesy:

May I not now ask which alternation I am to adopt—whether I must believe that a few years which have elapsed since you wrote me these letters have sufficed to make you reverse your opinion of my poems, or whether that opinion was even then ill-considered & expressed in stronger language than your critical judgment warranted?[15]

Being excluded from *Parnassus*, she complained, is "a public retraction" of his "extravagent admiration." With all due immodesty, she declared,

I felt as if I had won for myself by my own efforts a place in any collection of American poets, & I find myself treated with absolute contempt in the very quarter where I had been encouraged to build my fondest hopes.[16]

No reply to this letter has ever been found.

One writer on Emma Lazarus suggests that the *Parnassus* affair drove her away from the world of Lowell, Howells, and Emerson, and she came to embrace her "second phase," the Jewish phase, several years later. Another thinks her later phase came about much more suddenly.[17] Biographically, this is interesting speculation. Critically, we must admit that Lazarus's best poetry did come during her Jewish period, and, while some of her earlier poetry does have beauty and interest, the Brahmin in his mysterious way declined to immortalize what were, in retrospect, her lesser efforts.

V   *The End of the Matter*

If Emerson visited Lazarus in New York in 1875, as a notation in his memo books suggests,[18] he must have placated her, for the next year she visited the Emerson household and a fine time was had by all—as Ellen Emerson, who became Emma's correspondent, reports.[19] But *Parnassus* was never forgotten.

When Emerson died in May 1882 Lazarus published an appreciation in the July issue of the *Century*. As a personality, she writes, he was an individualist, a spirit, a philosopher, a lecturer, a poet. His idealism "stood erect and shining," a bulwark and a beacon against "the turmoil and greed of our modern life." He led his disciples by being exemplary. When, however, she discusses him as a critic and mentor of young writers, Lazarus's pained memories can be discerned. He was not "infallible": she could not agree with his low estimate of Shelley and Poe (the latter had also been excluded from *Parnassus*), and he had little or no knowledge of Heine, her own favorite German poet. Lazarus lays these critical weaknesses to his "strong religious bias" which "developed in him certain idiosyncrasies of taste and opinion." Above all, she comments, a young writer had to learn how to read Emerson's criticism properly. "He never acknowledged the receipt of works sent to him by authors, unless he could offer them encouragement." Yet, and here her sad memories find voice, "his praise . . . almost overpower[s] the recipient by its poetic hyperbole." Young writers, Lazarus says, were inspired to moments of exaltation, "almost . . . into immortality."[20] Older and wiser now, Lazarus seems to emphasize the "almost." She didn't, after all, make it into *Parnassus*.

She wrote a sonnet, dated May 20, 1884, published for the second anniversary of his passing. There is no record of her making a pilgrimage to Concord, as the sonnet implies, but if she did not make a physical journey thither, she certainly made a mental one:

TO R. W. E.
As when a father dies, his children draw
About the empty hearth, their loss to cheat
With uttered praise & love, & oft repeat
His all-familiar words with whispered awe,
The honored habit of his daily law,
Not for his sake, but their's whose feeble feet
Need still that guiding lamp, whose faith, less sweet,
Misses that tempered patience without flaw,
So do we gather round thy vacant chair,
In thine own elm-roofed, amber-rivered town,
Master & Father! For the love we bear,
Not for thy fame's sake, do we weave this crown,
And feel thy presence in the sacred air,
Forbidding us to weep that thou art gone.[21]

In a way, it was fortunate that master and pupil parted when they did. Always suspicious of political causes—even Abolition and the Civil War—Emerson would not have approved of Lazarus's later inflammatory pieces on behalf of persecuted Jewry. He preferred his Poet to be universal, to lead through—not in—the commonplace and the contemporary to cosmic beauty and truth. The later Emma Lazarus came to see the role of the Poet quite otherwise.

How, then, shall we summarize Emerson's effect on Lazarus? He was, first of all, a source of inspiration and pride to her. A Brahmin from the New England pantheon took an abiding interest in a little Jewish girl from New York! It is to Emerson's credit that he did so, and to Lazarus's that she kindled it. Second, she tried to follow his dicta about Nature, reading, imagery, diction, and such, but her temperament was not attuned to his ideals. Either she simply could not compose lyrics that consistently satisfied the *magister*, or, when she did, she could not recognize how much better they were than her low-grade, sentimental efforts. More than anything else, however, he stood as the old teacher who hovers in the back of the minds of all of us, demanding our best efforts always.

CHAPTER 4

"Pictures of Gods, Heroes, and Women"

UNLIKE that of the earlier volume, the title of Emma Lazarus's next book, *Admetus and other Poems* (1871),[1] does not really describe its contents. It should have read: *Myths, Lyrics, and Translations.* From Greek mythology she reworked the Admetus-Alcestis and the Orpheus stories, and from medieval legends she retold the tales of Lohengrin and Tannhäuser. Among the lyrics, she waxed somewhat autobiographical in a cycle of sixteen little poems entitled "Epochs" and typically sentimental in graveyard poems and nature pieces. Her translations represent a shift of interest from the French of Victor Hugo to the German of Goethe, but include a simple twelve-line "Song" by Heine.

We shall find that a new motif—that of the Poet Aspirant—gains prominence in *Admetus and Other Poems.* No doubt inspired by Emerson, Lazarus reveals a new self-consciousness as artist in poems about bards and, obliquely, about herself.

I The Myth of "Admetus"

As an endnote to her retelling of the four ancient legends in *Admetus and Other Poems*, of which the title poem is the first, Emma Lazarus felt compelled to print the following declaration:

> Note: In spite of my unwillingness to imply any possible belief of mine that the preceding unrhymed narratives can enter into competition with the elaborate poem of the author of "The Earthly Paradise," yet the similarity of subjects, and the imputation of plagiarism already made in private circles, induce me to remark that "Admetus" was completed before the "Love of Alcestis," and "Tannhäuser" before the "Hill of Venus." EMMA LAZARUS"
> (*Poems*, I, 126)

That this disclaimer was necessary reveals more about the lack of perspicacity among Lazarus's readers in those "private circles," and circles not so private, than it does about her habits of composition. For one notable example, William Dean Howells rejected "Admetus" for the *Atlantic* with this comment to Emerson: "It is so very plain an imitation in the manner of some of the Greekish poems of Tennyson, and all the Greekish poems of William Morris, that it is for that reason alone undesirable." [2] When Emerson rejoined that he could detect no Victorian echoes in "Admetus," he was more right than Howells. The editors of *Lippincott's* were untroubled by alleged imitation of the British poets: they published "Admetus" in September 1870, devoting thirteen pages to it.

The only connections between Lazarus's and Morris's poems are the accidents of subject and of chronology. Morris published *The Earthly Paradise*, containing "The Love of Alcestis," in April 1868. [3] By October 1868, Lazarus had sent the manuscript of "Admetus" to Emerson, and later revised it according to his general suggestions. A comparison of the two versions demonstrates that if she had read Morris's "The Love of Alcestis" at all before writing her own version, she learned from him what not to do. [4]

Morris wrote a long, fluid narrative in iambic pentameter couplets, but smoothness of verse never yet prevented tediousness, especially in a narrative poem. We must wade through long descriptions of Nature until we get to the first point of rising action: the coming of the god Apollo *incognito* to Admetus's feast. Then there is a tedious development of their friendship. Not until nearly half the poem is done does Alcestis make her appearance. The reason for her late coming is plain. Bound by the scheme of *The Earthly Paradise*—a cycle of stories in verse celebrating each month of the earthly year— Morris makes Apollo, the god of the sun, the hero of "The Love of Alcestis," because it is the June entry. [5] The ancient plot of the story itself becomes secondary to the primary place, in this version, of the Sun-god.

Lazarus, on the other hand, is writing a love story, and she does so with dash and drama. In the first place, "Admetus" is in blank verse, and we have already seen that in blank verse she writes with a verve of language and tone that she too often cannot get into her rhymed verse. Second, Lazarus does not allow tangential matters to delay the plot of Alcestis and Admetus.

In a rush to get to her love story, Lazarus's exposition plunges into the contest to determine the bridegroom of Alcestis:

He who could beard the lion in his lair,
To bind him for a girl, and tame the bear,
And drive these beasts before his chariot,
Might wed Alcestis.

(Poems, I, 59)

With such admirable, compact gracefulness Lazarus cuts through the introduction. She quickly establishes Apollo (here called Hyperion) as herdsman to King Admetus, leaves him in his subservient role waiting for the climax of events, and leaps to the scene in which Admetus first espies the gentle, beautiful, graceful Alcestis. Morris had set the encounter in a noisy gathering of hunters in the goddess Diana's house. Lazarus locates it in a quiet pretty forest alcove where Admetus, at the end of a hunting spree, comes upon her:

On a low bank she fondled tenderly
A favorite hound . . .
One arm with lax embrace the neck enwreathed
With polished roundness near the sleek, grey skin.

(Poems, I, 59–60)

Like any young man casting about for an opening speech to a beautiful damsel, Admetus asks her an inane question—the way out of the forest. She tells him, but again like any youth in these circumstances, he seeks a way of delaying his departure:

. . . . Still he tarried, and with sportsman's praise
Admired the hound and stooped to stroke its head,
And asked her if she hunted.

(Poems, I, 60)

Lazarus here accomplishes what Morris did not: she transcends the inevitable distance between myth and the modern reader and limns her characters with flesh-and-blood naturalness. They do not walk through the story like figures detached from a classical frieze.

Lazarus's description of Admetus winning the contest of the beasts takes a few lines; Morris's account sounds like a retelling of the story of Noah, as the animals parade two-by-two before Admetus's chariot. Morris halts the plot to give an elaborate description of the wedding. Lazarus tells us simply, "Admetus won Alcestis thus to wife," and they "lived a life blameless, beautiful." She is in a hurry to reach the crescendo of the story, where "sickness seized the king" and

> . . . Forlorn Alcestis sat
> Discouraged, with the face of desolation:
> The jealous gods would bind his mouth from speech,
> And smite his vigorous frame with impotence
> And ruin with bitter ashes, worms and dust,
> The beauty of his crowned, exalted head.
> He knew her presence,—soon he would not know,
> Nor feel her hand in his lie warm and close,
> Nor care if she were near him anymore. . . .
>
> (*Poems*, I, 63–64)

The deep affection, the sense of disappointment, the horror of waste of life and love are here dramatically suggested, and the understatement carries the drama and the reality. Not until Edwin Arlington Robinson's *Tristram* fifty years later do we get so realistic yet poetic a picture of love and desolation inspired by an ancient legend.

In "The Love of Alcestis," Morris has Apollo, the hero of the poem, come of his own accord into the dying king's chamber to reveal to the queen what the fates have already decreed: they will accept another life for that of Admetus. In "Admetus," because Lazarus has cast her as the hero, Alcestis is made to run in desperation to Hyperion in the fields to beg on her knees to give life to Admetus. Hyperion then descends into Hell to argue with the Fates, which gives Lazarus a chance to describe the Fates' Hades:

> . . . Wrapped in grim murk
> And darkness thick, the three gray women sat,
> Loose-robed and chapleted with wool and flowers,
> Purple narcissi round their horrid hair.
> Intent upon her task, the first one held
> The slender thread that at a touch would snap;
> The second weaving it with warp and wool
> Into strange textures, some stained dark and foul,
> Some sanguine-colored, and some black as night,
> And rare ones white, or with a golden thread
> Running throughout the web: the farthest hag
> With glistening scissors cut her sisters' work.
>
> (*Poems*, I, 66–67)

Rather than Tennyson or Morris, Howells should have heard echoes rising from Milton's Hell and the court of King Chaos in *Paradise Lost*. This picture of the Fates is so effective that we are made to fear that even Hyperion will be unsuccessful, but at his godlike tone "all

hell heard, and these three looked / And waited his request." To
which they reply:

> "What care we for the king? He is not worth
> These many words; indeed, we love not speech.
> We care not if he live, or lost such life
> As men are greedy for,—filled full with hate,
> Sins beneath scorn, and only lit by dreams,
> Or one sane moment, or a useless hope,—
> Lasting how long?—the space between the green
> And fading yellow of the grass they tread."
>
> *(Poems*, I, 68)

These are not pretty lines about life and death written by a neophyte
poseur: the sonorousness of epical blank verse sounds in them.

Lazarus sets the next scene in the king's chamber: he is deathly ill;
around him are his queen, parents, retainers, and the queen's
brother. In a dramatic sequence reminiscent of *Everyman*, Alcestis
asks in turn her brother, Admetus's parents, and his slaves to offer
themselves; each professes his readiness for death, but realistically
refuses to seek it, with reasons that are hard to controvert. The
brother says, "But if [my life] is little, no greater is the king's" (*Poems*,
I, 72). The aged couple reply, "Life is always life, / And death comes
soon enough to such as we" (*Poems*, I, 73). Refused by all Admetus's
near ones, Alcestis offers herself.

At this point, Admetus awakes and is appalled at Alcestis's sacrifice:

> " . . . Deemest thou that I accept the boon,
> Craven, like these my subjects? Lo, my queen,
> Is life itself a lovely thing,—bare life?
> And empty breath a thing desirable?
> Or is it rather happiness and love
> That make it precious to its inmost core?"
>
> *(Poems*, I, 79)

Admetus's speech may be a passion torn to tatters, but at least
Lazarus tried to instill passion into the story and the characters.
Morris does not. He gives to Admetus as cold and curt a eulogy for
Alcestis as Richard II bespoke for John of Gaunt, and leaves her dead.

Lazarus, however, is not finished. Abruptly, she shifts the scene.
While Alcestis is dying, saying goodbye to her baby son (always an
effective death scene), asking that he be brought up knowing "his
mother spoke with gods," outside her door Death waits. He is

accosted by Alcides (Hercules), who asks him for whom he is waiting. Death tells him, and Alcides tries to dissuade him, arguing that since the Fates had spared Admetus, let Death now spare Alcestis, the heroine queen. To which Death replies:

> "Behold, their smile is deadlier than their sting,
> And every boon of theirs is double-faced.
> Yea, I am gentler unto ye than these:
> I slay relentless, but when have I mocked
> With poisoned gifts, and generous hands that smite
> Under the flowers? for my name is Truth."
>
> *(Poems,* I, 78)

Death's speech is so effective in dignity and rectitude that all Alcides can do is declare war nevertheless. Alcides wins, Alcestis revives. Next morning, amidst "bright floods of sunny light," they see

> Afar upon the plain, Death fleeing thence.
> And at the doorway, weary, well-nigh spent,
> Alcides, flushed with victory.
>
> *(Poems,* I, 80)

The epilogue, with Alcides defeating Death in an all-night wrestling match that ends at dawn, recalls Jacob battling the dark Angel in Genesis 32. Twice more in this collection of poems Lazarus will be drawn to this allusion, identifying Jacob with the Poet Aspirant and the dark angel with all the obstacles the artist must overcome.

It is interesting to note that British comments on "Admetus" did not mention William Morris in connection with this poem at all. They compared Lazarus's treatment of the story to Robert Browning's retelling in *Balaustion's Adventure,* published the same year as Lazarus's volume. No question of plagiarism arises, only a question of comparative worth. And Emma Lazarus is found superior! The *Illustrated London News,* for example, commented, "In her treatment of the story of Alcestis and Admetus . . . she is far happier than Mr. Browning in his half adaptation of Euripides." [6] The reviewer of the *Westminster Review* launched himself against "admirers of Browning" to utter "something akin to blasphemy:" "In some points ["Admetus"] bear[s] comparison with 'Balaustion's Adventure.'" Waxing really courageous, this reviewer quoted a passage from the description of the forest where Admetus first sees Alcestis and opined that it is "thoroughly pastoral, and smells, as Shakespeare would say, of April and May." In one regard, however, *Westminster's* reviewer found Lazarus relatively weak. "We do not . . . find the same depth of philosophic reflection in her as in our own favorite poet." [7] The observation is an accurate one.

II *Portrait of a Bard: Orpheus*

Two of the remaining myths Lazarus retells in *Admetus and Other Poems* concern legendary bards, Orpheus and Tannhäuser. Not only do they offer Lazarus's beloved theme of love and catastrophe, but they also deal with her new motif, "The allegory of the true poet overcome by the 'gross and violent,' " as Arthur Zeiger has described it. [8] But if we look for realism in the depiction of the gross and violent, we shall not find it. Her hero-poets operate in a never-never land, among ghostly villains. Lazarus's world is still the ordered world of a genteel imagination. Her heroic masters of the lyre battle only mythic representatives of the gross and violent, like the Bacchantes, the acolytes of Bacchus who overcome Orpheus, and a fleshly Venus who in effect destroys Tannhäuser.

Orpheus is the story of a bard who twice loses his beloved. Once he is able to reclaim her from the dead, but the second time, she is lost eternally. On the basis of past performance, we might expect Lazarus to indulge in a paroxysm of pathos, overemphasized irony, and treacly elegy. To her credit we find that, except for certain passages, her control is firm. She writes in blank verse, which again proves to be her strength, although she hardly realized it. The beginning of her description of the wedding of Orpheus and Eurydice is in itself a wedding of sound and image:

> Laughter and dance, and sounds of harp and lyre
> Piping of flutes, singing of festal songs,
> Ribbons of flame from flaunting torches, dulled
> By the broad summer sunshine, there had filled
> Since high noon the pillared vestibules,
> The peristyles and porches, in the house
> Of the bride's father.
>
> (*Admetus*, 27)

Lazarus diverts our eye from joyous scene to joyous scene, controlling the impulsiveness of images with alliteration and balance of line. We are filled with sensuous delight and narrative expectancy.

When the plot carries the action to Hades, Lazarus turns once more to *Paradise Lost* for inspiration. When Orpheus awakens Eurydice to come back with him from Hell to Earth, he says:

> . . . Follow me
> From Darkness palpable [cf. "palpable obscure," *Paradise*
>   *Lost*, II, 406], to earth, to light,
> Of ample skies, and freshness of blown grass
> And rolling waters.
>
> (*Admetus*, 41)

Her equivalent of Satan, here named Ades, consort of Persephone, queen of the Underworld, is easily the best characterized. Like Milton, she found the villain an easier character to portray than her hero. In contrast to the effeminate Orpheus and languid Eurydice, Ades demonstrates strength and decisiveness. Self-confidence and tested experience, not empty egotism, produce this challenge to Orpheus:

> To reveal thyself the seer of gods,
> Not only through inspired ecstasy,
> But through a continent persistency,
> This never was accomplished by thy race,
> And thou must yet be tried.
>
> (*Admetus*, 47)

Indeed, Lazarus's characterization of the Bacchanates shows that evil carries more realistic drama than heroism. When the rioters try to convince Orpheus to let go of his dream of Eurydice after he lost her the second time, they say to him

> Here nymphs no whit less fair
> Are awaiting thee, with warm, caressing arms
> And loving eyes, lips fit for gods to kiss,
> And rosy shoulders, dimpling white and bare,—
> Pliant and graceful with innumerable charms,
> To sate thy heart with bliss.

Lazarus, again like Milton, had a problem in keeping the hero from sounding priggish in his innocence and morality. Milton, of course, succeeded to a large extent in the later books of his epic; Lazarus, however, leaves us with these lines of Orpheus:

> Hence, thou ignoble throng!
> Dare ye profane the splendid purity,

> The high nobility of morn, with rites
> Lewd and disgusting, and delirious song,
> Completing in clear sunshine, shamelessly
> Rude orgies of wild nights?
>
> (*Admetus*, 57)

The effect is nearly a caricature of outraged spinsterish innocence.

It is too bad that Lazarus could not compose stronger lines for Orpheus at this climactic moment, for he represents, from the age of yore, the Poet Aspirant. With Milton's shepherd-bard in "Lycidas," he refuses to sport, as it were, with Amaryllis in the shade, destining his talent only toward divine poems. It is a grand moment when he gives his life to the Bacchantes in defense of this ideal, but the lines on his lips when he does so are weak.

III   *Portrait of Another Bard: Tannhäuser*

A few months after she wrote "Orpheus" in December 1869, Lazarus turned to Sir Tannhäuser, the minstrel who gives in to bacchanalian love for a time. At the beginning of her version, Tannhäuser, "the greatest bard / Inspired with heavenly visions," is on his way to a gathering of minstrels. What these heavenly visions may be is not clear because he is stricken, rather, with agnostic, pagan doubts:

> How may my lyre
> Glorify these whose very life I doubt?
> The world is governed by one cruel God,
> Who brings a sword, not peace. A pallid Christ,
> Unnatural perfect, and a virgin cold,
> They give us for a heaven of living gods,
> Beautiful, loving, whose mere names were song . . . .
>
> (*Poems*, I, 82)

This passage reveals as much about Lazarus as about Tannhäuser. Never inspired by the God of the New Testament, not yet inspired by the God of the Old, Lazarus saw the Olympian deities as representing the Pierian spring of song. About them she could wax passionate, even indulging in dreams of wish fulfillment, as when Tannhäuser, bedeviled by thoughts Orpheus never conceived of, falls into the clutches of Venus, the goddess of fleshly love.

Venus at first is the cool goddess, whose passionate nature is only promised in the glory of her "unbraided and unfilleted" hair, and the radiant, exciting cestus girdle clasped "round her zone." She leads Tannhäuser up the mountain; she climbing like a gazelle, he like a panting stallion, "wild eyes fixed/Upon her brightness." Once Lazarus delivers them on top the Venusberg, she describes Venus as a

> very woman now,
> Fantastic, voluble, affectionate
> And jealous of the vague, unbodied air,
> Exacting, penitent, and pacified,
> All in a breath.
>
> (*Poems*, I, 89)

As if this were not wish fulfillment enough, Lazarus dwells on a sensual heaven that answers every teen-ager's fantasy:

> From revelry to revelry [Tannhäuser] passed,
> Craving more pungent pleasure momently,
> And new intoxications, and each hour
> The siren goddess answered his desires.
>
> (*Poems*, I, 90)

What this flesh-pot existence means to the minstrel is indicated when

> . . . his lyre he flung
> Recklessly forth, with vows to dedicate
> His being to herself
>
> (*Poems*, I, 88)

rather than to poesy.

After a number of years, Tannhäuser catches a reflection of his once-handsome face, now ugly with dissolution. Now he hears once more the call of the lyre and proposes to Venus that they end the liaison and remain good friends. The ensuing scene gives Lazarus the opportunity to launch into quite startling images of the woman scorned. First, Venus tries to dissuade him with the pouting-girl gambit:

> With girlish simpleness of folded hands,
> Auroral blushes, and sweet, shamefast mien.
>
> (*Poems*, I, 91)

This doesn't work. Next, she tries the role of the Piteous Woman:

> See I am kneeling, and I kiss thy hands—
> In pity, look on me.

Tannhäuser remains unmoved.

> Then she . . . rose, dilating over him,
> And sullen clouds veiled all her rosy limbs,
> Unto her girdle, and her head appeared,
> Refulgent, and her voice rang wrathfully:
> "Have I cajoled and flattered thee till now,
> To lose thee thus! How wilt thou make escape?
> *Once being mine, thou art forever mine*:
> Yea, not my love, but my poor slave and fool."
>
> (*Poems*, I, 92; Lazarus's italics)

Astounded, Tannhäuser cries, "Help me, O Virgin Mary," and with the utterance of this prayer, the Venusberg vanishes.

Tannhäuser finds himself once more upon the road, and now becomes a traveling penitent. He tells his story to the local priest, who sends him to the Bishop, who sends him to the Cardinal, who sends him to the Pope. Along the way, he meets a shepherd boy, who, taking him for a holy man, gives him food and drink. Tannhäuser by chance sees the boy's rude guitar, and the boy makes a quick apology for its primitiveness. To which Tannhäuser replies:

> " . . . Whoso hath
> The art to make this speak is raised thereby
> Above all loneliness or grief or fear."
>
> (*Poems*, I, 111)

He admits his own lyre is "lost! lost! forever lost!"

Resuming his search for surcease from the pangs of his experience, Tannhäuser is tormented by the fact that no one has yet been able to give him absolution and by the fear that Venus' curse may yet prevail. He reaches the Pope, and after countless delays, gets to see him. But the Pope considers the sin so great that forgiveness is impossible. The Pope intones harshly:

> "Yea, sooner shall my pastoral rod branch forth
> In leaf and blossom, and green shoots of spring,
> Than Christ will pardon thee."
>
> (*Poems*, I, 119)

So Tannhäuser takes to the road again, and seeks God outside of "all forms, all priests." [9] He prays all night amidst soulful torment. Next morning,

> Shivering with fever, helpless he arose,
> But with a face divine, ineffable,
> Such as we dream the face of Israel,
> When the Lord's wrestling angel, at gray dawn,
> Blessed him, and disappeared.
>
> *(Poems, I, 121)*

As used here for the second time, this biblical allusion refers directly to the conflict in the artist between art and reality.

The end of Tannhäuser is now predictable. Ill, he is taken in by the shepherd boy with the rude lyre and is honored by him; in the lad's care he dies. The epilogue recounts that the Pope's rod one day unaccountably did bring forth green leaves. *(Poems, I, 126)*

Lazarus's moral is clear. Tannhäuser is a poet who has made a wrong choice. He permits sensuality—call it a symbol of the demands inevitably made by the real world—to destroy his divine gift. But there is always the chance of spiritual rebirth after this spiritual death. Though Tannhäuser never regains the divine song, he does regain something of his former spiritual condition. That this is found acceptable in the upper world is signified by the sprouting of green leaves from a dead stick.

As a retelling of the medieval tale, "Tannhäuser" holds its place among more famous versions. Although Arthur Zeiger finds that it "loses humor (Heine), passion (Wagner), poignancy (Morris),—a sorry trade," [10] other critics found it more competent. The reviewer in the *Galaxy* found it "finer than Morris' 'Hill of Venus'" from *The Earthly Paradise*, [11] and the reviewer in the *Nation* also classed it favorably with Morris's version. [12] The critic in *Lippincott's* found it "less melodious, but more dramatic; more forcible [sic], more masculine," than "The Hill of Venus." [13]

For all his lyricism, Morris robbed the story of its meaning and drama. In his version, Walter, the hero, is not a poet, merely a stock Romantic figure afflicted with the conventional malaise. The involvement of the Pope, therefore, is out of proportion to the crime of dallying with Venus. Unlike Lazarus, Morris never conveys a feeling of concern for his plot or characters. Indeed, there is no characterization to leaven the dexterity of the verse. "The Hill of Venus" is merely

an exercise in versifying. In comparison, Lazarus's concern for narrative and characterization emphasizes her tendency to the dramatic.
Above all, her hero is a poet, and his physical dissipation and spiritual
rise give a special mission to Lazarus's poem that is lacking in Morris's
pretty, but inconsequential, version. Again the differences are so
great that it is difficult to see what so exercised the readers of
Lazarus's narratives that she was forced to deny plagiarism.

IV   Epochs of a Tormented Girl

In February 1871 Emma Lazarus completed a cycle of poems
called "Epochs" which represent for the first time in her canon the
metamorphosis of true personal passion into poetry. Two events have
been suggested as the stimuli for these poems dealing with life's
varied moments. One critic, Albert Mordell, believes that "Emma
had loved and lost, and the impact was stunning. . . . Out of her
experience she made an allegory of the despair and recovery of the
human soul." [14] The unresponsive object of her love, if it ever
existed, has since been identified as her cousin, Washington Nathan,
to whom she dedicated "Lohengrin." [15] Zeiger, on the other hand,
disposes of Mordell's thesis as a Freudian fantasy. He offers as the real
event inspiring the writing of "Epochs" Emerson's letter following
the murder of Washington Nathan's father, Benjamin, on July 28,
1870. Emerson had read about the event—a rather famous affair in
New York, during which Washington was suspected of parricide—
and on August 19, 1870, wrote to Emma a note of condolence. This
letter, Zeiger claims, gave her the outline of "Epochs." [16] Emerson's
note, however, is a brief and rather conventional encouragement to
keep a stiff upper lip. It might possibly have suggested a stoic ending
to "Epochs," but it hardly outlined a program of life.

These critics also differ on the meaning of Lazarus's headnote for
the series; a quotation from Emerson, it reads: "The epochs of our life
are not the visible facts, but in the silent thought by the wayside as we
walk." Mordell advises us that this "is not the theme"; the quotation is
"meant to throw the reader off his guard as to her personal humiliation and disappointment." [17] On a less personal basis, Zeiger believes
that Lazarus found in Emerson's statement justification that mental
experience, dreams, and thoughts, are proper sources of poetry. [18]
One thing is certain: the headnote represents a counterstatement to
Emerson's personal admonition to "detect the deity that still challenges you under all the gross and vulgar." With it Lazarus justifies

the total avoidance of the gross and vulgar in these poems to search for a deity in revery.

The plot of the cycle concerns a young woman, referred to only in the third person, who apparently suffers a disappointment so deep and sudden that she calls it a "surprise." She descends into torpor, but then slowly, painfully rises from it to achieve a mental equilibrium. On one hand, some of the passages contain so deep a personal sound that it is not difficult to conjecture that they come from an emotional trauma. On the other hand, the motif and moods are so familiar by now that the depth of expression may be due only to artistic improvement.

To give the disappointment greater feeling and irony, Lazarus begins with the epoch of "Youth." As in Emerson and Wordsworth, Nature in youth is sensuous and careless:

> The mystic winged and flickering butterfly,
> A human soul, that hovers, giddily
> Among the garden of earth's paradise,
> Nor dreams of fairer fields or loftier skies.
>
> (*Poems* I, 40–1)

However, life demands a fall from the paradise of youth. In the next epoch, entitled "Regret," she pines "for the lost beauty of gracious morn." The soul is caught between "dream[s] of the future void of grief and pain /And mus[ing] upon the past, in reveries" (*Poems*, I, 42). Encapsulating her life like the poet of the "Ode on Intimations," "serene was morning," but as the day rolls on, clouds "rose in the west" and "the sunshine dies."

The cataclysm of love unrequited breaks like a sudden storm around her:

> And all the while the dreadful thunder breaks,
> Within the hollow circle of the hills,
> With a gathering might, that angry echoes wakes,
> And earth and heaven with unused clamor fills.
> O'erhead, still flame those strange electric thrills.
> A moment more,—behold! yon bolt struck home
> And over ruined fields the storm hath come.
>
> (*Poems*, I, 43)

If Lazarus had Byron's storm in *Childe Harold's Pilgrimage* in mind, she sadly did not equal the inspiration in her verse. Unlike Byron,

Lazarus does not symbolize her own inner turmoil in the external storm. She finds no release, no abandon, no participation in the cataclysm. The soul is merely stunned (section V—"Surprise"), not purged, by the storm. "Self–pitying grief" reflects a heart that "is a cold dead stone" (*Poems*, I, 44). The nadir of the sad cycle of inner life comes in section VIII, "Loneliness," the worst mood of all. After "all stupor of surprise hath passed away," she finds herself mummified, "the heart eaten out," alienated.

Thus far a spiritual death has been allegorized. A spiritual rebirth awaits. Rebirth is aided by a new persona in "Epochs," a friend who makes an appearance in section IX, "Sympathy":

> Such a one brought rest [to the aggrieved heroine]
> And bade her lay aside her doubts and fears,
> While the hard pain dissolved in blessed tears.
>
> (*Poems*, I, 47)

Had Emma Lazarus achieved the fame of Emily Dickinson, hordes of avid students would have searched for "such a one," but there is at present no extant biographical hint.

The experience ennobled and strengthened her. Now she can discover in herself a wisdom that can say

> There is the deeper pathos in the mild
> And settled sorrow of the quiet eyes
> Than in the tumults of the anguish wild. . . .
>
> (*Poems*, I, 48)

Such aphoristic lines are new in Emma Lazarus's work. While they do not have the telegraphy of Dickinson, they convey the quiet, stately pithiness of the homey poems of Longfellow, from whom Lazarus drew in other connections in *Admetus and Other Poems*.

"Hope" (section XI) springs eternal once more, and if grief came suddenly as a storm, "How may joy dawn?" "May the light break with splendor of surprise?" (*Poems*, I, 49). The beautifully alliterated phrase denies the former sad meaning of "surprise" and engulfs it with a new-found "splendor." With the philosophic mind (and poetic echoes) of the poet of the "Ode on Intimations" again Lazarus perceives

> Though the glory and the joy be fled,
> 'Tis much her own endurance to have weighed,
> And wrestled with God's angels, unafraid.
>
> (*Poems*, I, 50)

This is the third time in *Admetus* that this biblical image thrusts itself into the poetry. As in "Tannhäuser," it serves again as a symbol of the artist rising from a severe crisis.

"Victory" (section XV) over the dread angel is not accomplished so quickly. The grief has been so sharp that death will not "prove an all–unwelcome guest" (*Poems*, I, 52), but only after she has traversed, as Robert Frost would say, the miles she must go before she sleeps. With this reconciliation, the poet can conclude on a note of "Peace" (section XVI) and not only peace, but aspiration to enter the world of spirit and imagination. Reprising an early quatrain—

> The mystic-winged and flickering butterfly
> A human soul, that drifts at liberty,
> Ah! who can tell to what strange paradise
> To what undreamed-of fields and lofty skies!
>
> (*Poems*, I, 53)

The butterfly no longer is attached to "earth's paradise," as in section I, but is "at liberty"; no longer aspires to fields and skies already dreamt, but to realms so lofty that they have not yet been dreamed of. With this, the allegory of the Poet Aspirant ends.

We need not, then, worry too much about the personal "truth" of the allegory. The crisis in the poet's life might have been experienced or imagined, but let us not forget that imagining is experiencing as well. And deeply felt, too, to judge from the pithiness of verse, in which Emma Lazarus expressed old moods as well as new feelings. If some of "Epochs" is clearly the work of the immature girl versifier of 1867, more of it is the expression of a woman poet who no longer merely plays at versifying.

V *"Dreams Are the Solidest Facts . . ."*

A number of the poems in *Admetus and Other Poems* that follow "Epochs" are typified by one entitled "Dreams," written on April 30, 1867. Four dreams are each symbolized by a different flower: lilies represent the "eternal source of pleasure and joy"; roses equal love; laurels symbolize the "much buried, much lamented, much forgot"; finally, poppies tell us "all these were dreams of vanity." The upshot of all this dreaming is—

> He dreams it may be good to dream no more,
> And life has nothing like Dream's deathless
>   sleep.
>
> (*Admetus*, 155–56)

If this poem had appeared in Lazarus's first book, no more need be said about it, for it is of a piece with those written at that time. But she selected it for inclusion in *Admetus*, after several years of writing poetry and of being the beneficiary of Emerson's criticism. Placing it almost immediately after the Emerson-inspired "Epochs" cycle suggests that "Dreams" announces the way Lazarus thought to fulfill Emerson's notions of symbolism, the role of the poet, and the world in which he exists. Emerson placed the roots of the poetic experience in Nature and used Nature's language to transform reality into awareness.

Lazarus, however, simply misinterpreted all this. Transcendence to her meant entering a dream-world. The word "dreams," indeed, becomes the most important and frequently used noun in the remaining lyrics of *Admetus and Other Poems*. But to see dreams as the world of the poet is to deny Nature entirely as the source of both experience and poetic language. Under these circumstances, Nature becomes an encumbrance and loses its usefulness as a metaphor. Without the reservoir of natural symbolism to call upon for her verse, Lazarus tends to write direct descriptions of emotion. Such a method, however, often robs her verse of the drama of true emotion poetically expressed. Expression must inevitably become imprecise and approximate, and the experience sounds posed and pretended.

An example of this notion of writing poetry (it cannot be called a theory) is a poem called "Reality" (dated May 1869). For a headnote Lazarus quotes Thoreau: "Hold fast to your most indefinite waking dream. Dreams are the solidest facts that we know" (*Admetus*, 179). Thoreau was the most precise of nature-inspired writers, the most sensuous in his descriptions of natural life and what nature meant to him. The dreams which become real to him were engendered by sounds, sights, and smells and have a correspondence with them. It is certainly a misunderstanding of Thoreau to begin a poem attributed to his inspiration "Celestial hopes and dreams", and avoid throughout the entire poem the use of a single concrete image of Nature!

In this poem, however, we find a clue to why Lazarus reached for this kind of transcendence: it was an escape from reality. At one point she refers to a legend about a youth who seized a god that could assume all shapes, but the youth held on until the one Truth (never specified) emerged. "We [too] seize the god in youth," she says, but then "ambition, folly, gain" loosen our hold on truth:

> We grow more wise, we say,
> And work for worldly ends and mock a dream.
> Alas! all life's glory and its gleam,.
> With that have fled away.
>
> (*Admetus*, 180)

The echoes are once again from Wordsworth's "Ode." The "Ode"
seemed to Lazarus to exemplify a compatible approach to poetry.
Regardless of what Wordsworth may have intended, Lazarus seems
to have read the poem as proving that Nature may be the initial
setting for the act of imagination, but ultimately gives way to something mental—the "philosophic mind," Wordsworth called it. Thus,
in "The Garden of Adonis," a poem suggested, as Lazarus notes, by
Spenser's *Faerie Queene* (III, vi, stanzas 39–40), Nature serves merely as a sign that death may die. Nature represents a process

> . . . called Change
> And all it does is beautiful and strange.
> It is but Change that lays our darlings low,
> And, though we doubt and fear, foresakes them not.
>
> (*Admetus*, 171)

Like Whitman in "Song of Myself," Lazarus postulates that change of
composition within the cycle of Nature is all that death really is. But
even this is not the final answer. In the last stanza of this poem,
Lazarus, *a propos* of no motif heretofore presented, suddenly asks:

> And dreams? What dreams were ever lost and gone,
>   But wandering in strange lands be found again?
>   . . .
> And he is blind who doth not know or see,
> And praise the gods for immortality.
>
> (*Admetus*, 173)

Though the dream-world offers permanence, constancy, and a
species of idealism, yet for Lazarus it did not often offer good poetry.
In such a world, her language becomes trite, inverted, a prey to
hackneyed rhymes. Imagery becomes amorphous and unfocused—
and why should it not, arising as it does in a state of revery that is
amorphous and unfocused.

VI   *Graveyard Poems*

Two graveyard poems included in *Admetus and Other Poems* were
inspired this time not by foreign sentimentalists, but by a native one,
Henry Wadsworth Longfellow. The first, entitled "In a Swedish
Graveyard," is tritely sentimental. The other, "In the Jewish Synagogue at Newport," has richer meditative tone. Both were written in
1867.

What caught Lazarus's fancy in Longfellow's *Rural Life in Sweden*,
from which she quotes in a headnote, is the custom of placing a
lighted taper in the hands of the dying at the moment of expiration
and burying them with head westward (*Admetus*, 165). The candle
fascinates her:

> Each one held a lit taper when dying:
> Where had vanished the fugitive flame?
> With his love, and his joy, and his sighing,
> Alas! and his youth and his name.
>
> (*Admetus*, 165)

As the "living stands o'er him and dreameth," the poet wonders
whether the dead "dream of the strife and the crown" (how could she
avoid thinking of Gray's graveyard "Elegy"?) and "what dreams came
to them in their living." How ironic dreaming comes to be, when one
contemplates "the poor little lights . . . flickering faint" on the
features, giving them the appearance of life. Piously, she concludes
with the uncertain hope that "utter darkness and sleep may be best,"
after all (*Admetus*, 166–67).

The other graveyard poem, "In the Jewish Synagogue at Newport," takes on greater significance because of three factors. For the
first time Lazarus transcends pretended personal loss in death to
ruminate upon the wider significance of it. Second, Death is seen as a
factor in history. Third, for the first time Lazarus confronts a Jewish
subject for a poem.

Obviously, her poem is to be read as a companion-piece to Longfellow's "The Jewish Cemetery at Newport." Inspired by the age of the
cemetery and the past glory of the Hebrew nation, Longfellow had
eulogized the contribution of this people to civilization. No matter
how laudable he may be in his poem and no matter that he knew that
remnants of this nation still survived, this righteous Gentile wrote a
eulogy of the Jewish people: "The dead nations [he concludes,] never
rise again."

The Touro Synagogue in Newport was built with the aid of the Lazarus family's own Spanish-Portuguese Congregation in New York. Its worshipers followed the Sephardic ritual of her own tradition. But in its emptiness Emma saw the Jewish destiny in precisely the same way as Longfellow did. What is more significant is not only the historical perspective, but also the sense of distance this Jewish-born poet establishes—the impersonality, the dispassionate objectivity of her review of the highlights of the history of "these lone exiles of a thousand years. / [Driven] from their fair sunrise land that give them birth". She sees them only as a "relic of the days of old." She recalls "the patriarch and his flocks," and "the slaves of Egypt,— omens, mysteries—/ Dark fleeing hosts by flaring angels led." She pauses to note the giving of the Law and the climax of Jewish history, Solomon's reign. But these glories are merely reveries of remembrance of things past. From these reveries

> Alas! we wake: one scene alone remains—
> The exiles by the streams of Babylon.
>
> (*Admetus*, 160)

Exile and the dead past dominate the poem, symbolized by the little-used synagogue. Its holiness today is merely a concession to history:

> Nathless the sacred shrine is holy yet
> With its lone floors where reverent feet once trod.
> Take off your shoes as by the burning bush,
> Before the mystery of Death and God.
>
> (*Admetus*, 161)

The dead nations, as Longfellow had said, never rise again—in July 1867.

The irony is all too obvious: in a decade and a half, Lazarus will reverse herself entirely. She will call for a rebirth of the Jewish nation; she will envision the end of the exile and the return to "the fair sunrise land"; she will throw her heart into a cause that intends to defy history. And, incidentally, the inspiration will cleanse her poetry of brittle fashion and platitude.

VII *Love Songs*

In precisely the same years she was writing poems of melancholy, she wrote two delightful pieces—flecks of gold amid the mica. The

first is a departure from Walt Whitman, whom, she reported to
Emerson on June 27, 1868, she had been reading.[19] The second is a
ballad, "Marjorie's Wooing".

That "Out of the Cradle Endlessly Rocking" is perhaps Whitman's
greatest lyric has long been recognized. Evidently Lazarus thought
so, too, for she fashioned her poem called "Idyl" after it. The story in
"Out of the Cradle" tells of a boy already heeding the call of poetry,
watching two birds. They build a nest, but the female bird disappears
and the male bird trills arias of lament to the moon, the land, and the
sea. But she does not return, and the young bard-to-be from this
learns the fact of delicious death. Henceforth, his singing will echo
the bird's lament.

In Lazarus's poem, there are also two birds and the young poet
observing, listening. On a day drenched in sunshine, in woods where
"the swallows made twitter incessant," at a moment when nature
made "living divine," she sees two gray robins. The male bird "sang
to [the female bird] tenderest love-songs":

> And his song came forth clearer and clearer,
> With each passionate musical note;
> Like the ripple of silvery waters,
> It gushed from his beautiful throat.
> His whole little bird-soul he offers—
> Ah! she listens to him as he sings:
> Then he ceases awaiting her answer
> With bright eyes and with quivering wings.
>
> (*Admetus*, 189–90)

Here is the perfect opportunity for another descent into melancholy
passages on the transiency of life, on the eternality of love-in-death,
the themes one expects in a Lazarus poem of 1868. But no! she diverts
from Whitman, indeed, from her own usual inclinations, and ends on
a happy (if fairy-tale) note. Like the boy in Whitman's poem, the
young poet here, too,

> Stood awaiting it, breathless
> For his song was too sweet to disdain.
> Till it came, little notes full of gladness,
> With a plaintive and tender refrain.
> And the songs died away in the distance
> And the forest alone heard the rest,
> As the two little lovers flew upward
> To build them together a nest.
>
> (*Admetus*, 190)

The meter of "Idyl" is anapestic trimeter, with a feminine ending in the odd lines, pure anapest in the even ones. She transformed the meter of action into a delicate instrument for composing a love poem, indeed a love poem about a love song. "One of Emma's few happy and uninhibited efforts," Zieger called it.[20]

The same can be said of "Marjorie's Wooing," dated December 25, 1867, a surprisingly early date for this accomplished union of theme and technique. The poem is actually a ballad, a little love story about Kenneth and Marjorie, told mainly in dialogue, like the old English and Scottish ballads. The meter is irregular but recognizable common meter; the rhyme scheme in each stanza is the conventional *abcb*. Refrains begin each stage of Kenneth's wooing, and repetitions dot the poem here and there in the old style. The whole combination is such a stunning achievement in this genre that one magazine printed the entire poem as part of its review. The last three stanzas give a sense of the whole:

> "Marjorie, Marjorie, if I should say
> That I was nobled, and titled, and grand
> Lord of the woods, and the castle, and park
> Lord of the acres of corn o'er the land?"
>
> Dropping a courtesy, the little lass said,
> "Still should I love you and ever be true;
> But if you found me too lowly and poor,
> I should bid farewell and go die for you."
>
> "Marjorie, darling I tell you then,
> This is the truth, and the land is mine,
> And the castle, the park, and vessel far off,
> And whatever is mine, is thine, dear, thine!"
>
> (*Admetus*, 170)

Happiness is not often an inspirational emotion for Emma Lazarus. Poems describing joy are so infrequent, and even then so rarely realized as experience, that when they do come they dazzle by contrast.

VIII *Faustian Poet*

The longest translation by far that Emma Lazarus published in *Admetus and Other Poems* was of the "Dedication," "Prologue in the Theatre," and Part I, scene i of Goethe's *Faust*. She apparently chose these passages because in them Goethe concerns himself with the problems of Art and the profession of the Poet. Thus, as an appendix to her own poems on hese subjects, the translation forms a kind of coda.

In the very first quatrain of the "Dedication," Goethe seems to call to her over the span of decades. He equates "dream," Lazarus's currently favorite exponent, with the ethereal goal of poetizing, currently her major theme:

> O hovering forms, ye come to me once more,
> Ye whom I saw in youth with troubled eyes.
> Do I believe this dream as heretofore?
> Shall I essay to grasp it, ere it flies?
>
> (*Admetus*, 199)

Then, in the "Prologue," the poet intones a panegyric to his calling by means of a series of grandiloquent rhetorical questions, which he answers with a single resounding declaration:

> Who calls the individual to share
> The universal consecrating prayer,
> With its celestial tones? . . .
> Who scatters aside
> Upon the loved one's path, fair buds of spring? . . .
> Who can ensure to dwellers on the earth.
> Olympus, and with gods can meet and rest?
> Man's power in the poet manifest!
>
> (*Admetus*, 206)

Emma Lazarus's sentiments exactly.

In Part I, scene i of his work, Goethe wrote a dialogue between Faust as the Master Poet and his servant Wagner as the Poet Aspirant that seems actually to sublimate whatever inner fears of mediocrity Emma Lazarus may have experienced during her correspondence with Emerson. With which one does she belong—will she fly with Faustian grandeur in her verse, or will she remain forever earth-bound, tortured by her limitations, sighing with poor Wagner:

> Good Lord! but art is long, and life is short,
> Oft in my critical pursuits, my head
> And heart are both oppressed. How difficult
> To gain the wherewithal to reach aright
> The fountain-head! When we are but halfway,
> Poor devils, we must die!
>
> (*Admetus*, 218-9)

In Lazarus's rendering of Goethe's German, we begin to see two general traits of her method of translation which will carry to the end of her career. First, because of nineteenth-century practice and her own way of expressing herself in verse, she retains archaic usage; but this usage most of the time does not jar the modern ear because she immerses it in a more colloquial expression than even her poetry often contains. Second, she is not afraid to insinuate her own interpretation of the spirit of the original into her translation.

This translation from *Faust* represents Lazarus's first intimate relationship with dramatic form, and it happened to be a work of a Romantic poet. Goethe's touch of influence would emerge presently, when Lazarus wrote *The Spagnoletto* in 1876, and the tragedy *The Dance to Death* in 1880. There we will see the Romantic excess, the flamboyance, the broadness of action and of characterization that she first saw here in Goethe's *Faust*.

IX   Admetus and Other Poems *in the Lazarus Canon*

No set of poems until *Songs of a Semite* in 1882 has the importance of *Admetus and Other Poems*. In it, Lazarus comes of age, despite all the shortcomings that we have discussed. In the first place, poetry is no longer dalliance to her, but a mission. The tone of sentimentality and unreality still predominates, but it is now balanced by a self-confidence of manner, an insight into psychology, an understanding of emotion that her previous poetry did not have. The book is a turning point after which even the most trite lyrical efforts take on a seriousness and poise that beguile us into reading her verse with attention, if not with admiration.

CHAPTER 5

Things Lyrical and Dramatic

DURING the ten years that followed the publication of her second
book of poems, *Admetus and Other Poems,* in 1871, Emma
Lazarus contributed dozens of poems to popular magazines, like
Lippincott's and *Scribner's.* Evidently she was considered gifted, to
judge from the frequency of her appearance, although the themes of
these efforts are dreaming, the transiency of time, love, death, the
cycle of nature—all so familiar in spirit and imagery that they sound
nearly automatic. Modern standards of poetry may dim her achieve-
ments, but as far as her readership then was concerned she had the
ability to gild what oft was thought and oft expressed.

On the other hand, her widening gaze turned once in a while from a
constant setting of Nature to that of the city, from the lyrical to the
dramatic in the form of a monologue and of a play. Perhaps the most
significant new feature of these years was her turn from translating
only favorite European poets to translating (albeit from German
versions) poetry by medieval Hebrew poets. From the latter moments we may date the beginning of her final phase. But that story
will occupy our attention in later chapters. Here we shall consider the
poetry derived from conventional sources and inspired by standard
emotions.

I   *The Familiar Reprised*

A typical example is "Rosemary" (*Lippincott's,* May 1872, pp.
542–43), wherein Lazarus offers lines as insipid and devoid of originality as these:

> Let me remember—for on such a day
> 'Tis sadder to forget than to recall!
> The perfect fulness of the golden May
> Holds earth and heaven in its subtle thrall . . .

and then redeems herself with lines made attractive by enjambment
and a vernacular language that freshens the old thought:

> Grief dies not, but grows part of the great soul:
> Though many an outstretched hand with gentle might
> At first may move her, yet as the seasons roll
> She slowly, surely learns how weak and slight
> Is every outward hold. . . .

Zeiger hears the transcendental echo of Emerson;[1] but on a lower level, we hear the elegaic tone of Gray, the blithe imprecision of Shelley, and the portentous stride of Wordsworth.

"Rosemary," it may be noted, was published in May and reflects a mood of sadness contrasted to the month of May. Lazarus liked to publish appropriate seasonal poems to order, as it were. Thus, a few months later, in November, she publishes "Expectations" (*Lippincott's*, November 1872, pp. 587–88), which begins with a description of "wintry fields left bare to skies unkind," jumps to "the pleasure of spring" yielding "white flowered orchards . . . [and] rainbows above where late the rain-cloud was," and continues with the conventional beauty of "a morn of June." Finally, as the climax of the poem, November becomes a harbinger

> Of death and winter and swift-coming change,
> A brighter dawn, a brighter April-tide. . . .

These seasonal announcements seemed to become nearly programmatic. In April 1875, *Lippincott's* published her "March Violet" (pp. 481–82); in May, she followed up with its sequel, "Spring Joy" (p. 570).

In "The Winds" (*Lippincott's*, October 1875), Lazarus combines the fable of the seasons with the symbolism of the four quadrants of the compass. It is almost inevitable that Shelley's "Ode to the West Wind" should exercise influence on this autumn poem, in theme, touches of imagery, and the use of *terza rima*. Lazarus begins with the South Wind, equivalent to late spring:

> . . . . This mild wind is he
> Painted with cloud-crowned head and floating hair,
> Gray beard, gray wings, gray raiment shadowy.

This is a fructive time, however, for in the rain "grief dissolve[s] in mist of memories" (p. 438). Shelley's voice becomes sharper, naturally, when Lazarus identifies, as Shelley did, the West Wind with "the spirit of Autumn." The soul is dormant during this season, and Lazarus wonders

> . . . why tarrieth she
> With idle hands, above a mound of clay?
> Waken her thou, her inspiration be;
>
> As the dry leaves thou scatterest on the way,
> Her withered fancies clinging still to death,
> Disperse, and chant with her a bolder lay. (p. 439)

The North, equated with night and winter, is that death, but as usual in this type of poem, "The earth lies cold and dumb, awaiting dawn" (p. 440). The dawn is symbolized by the East Wind of March:

> Light March skies dappled with white streaks and flakes,
> Dim, faded sunshine like the first faint smile
> Of one who after grievous ill awakes
>
> To life and love again. . . . (p. 440)

Inspired by Shelley's query, "If winter comes, can spring be far behind?" Lazarus replies, Certainly not! And when finally July comes, "Earth, sea, and heaven and windless air breathe peace" (p. 440).

The theme of transiency of time is not restricted to nature poems. It marks a tandem she called "Arabesque" and "Grotesque," published in the *Galaxy* in July and December 1877, respectively. A search for a connection to Poe's *Tales of the Grotesque and Arabesque* yields nothing, except the titles of fantasy. Lazarus's "Arabesque" is a reverie set in old Granada amid

> Brilliant-colored, Moorish scenes
> Mosques and crescents, pages, queens. . . .
>   . . .
> Here in Lindarxa's bower
> The immortal roses bloom . . .
> Where fair Lindaraxa dwelt
> Flits the bat on velvet wings. . . .
> Moonbeams kiss the floor with light
> Where she knelt. . . .
>
>   (*Poems*, I, 155–56)

The passage of time as well as the departure of King Boabdil destroyed this Paradise. The last stanza, with the help of Tennyson's *In Memoriam*, expresses her recognition of Time's power:

> Vanished like the wind that blows,
> Whither shall we seek their trace
>   On earth's face?
> The gigantic wheel of fate,
> Crushing all things soon or late,
>   Now a race,
> Now a single life o'erruns,
> Now a universe of suns,
>   Now a rose.
>
>   (*Poems*, I, 157)

Perhaps the intricacy of the prosody and rhyme scheme of this poem, reflecting the intricacy of Moorish art and architecture, served as another reason for calling the poem "Arabesque."

"Grotesque" was "suggested by a visit to the Castellani Collection in Rome," writes Lazarus in a headnote. (The visit had to be vicarious, however; she did not leave America until May 1883.) To the theme of Time Lazarus here adds the theme of the Artist. The plot of the poem imagines the statues coming to life at the end of the day and recalling the days of yore when they were gods and goddesses. The chief speaker is Dionysus, the god of wine and poetry. All day, he complains, he stands

> Stretching forth, to greet and bless,
>   My right hand.
> No one offers me a prayer;
> The barbarians stop and stare,
>   And pass by.

His despair is not serious, only conventional, and ends on a hopeful note:

> And I knew [the worshiper's] heart was mine;
> And I felt that Circumstance,
>   Time, and Chance,
> Are but shadows; still the same,
> Leaps the soul of youth, like flame,
>   At a glance
> Knowing, worshipping the god
> Of the joy-inspiring rod
>   And the wine.
>
>   (*Galaxy*, 24 [December 1877], p. 771)

The themes of the Artist and the irony of life find less sanguine expression in a poem on the death of Beethoven, titled "Comoedia,"

published in the *Independent* on July 26, 1877. The magazine turned
over its entire front page to this long blank-verse poem. The theme is
derived from Beethoven's last words, reported in the poem's headnote: "*Plaudite, amici, comoedia finita est*" (Applaud, my friends, the
comedy is ended). The story tells of Beethoven's sacrifices on behalf
of his nephew, Carl, for which he was compensated by Carl's cruel
selfishness and ingratitude, and finally by the great composer's loss
of hope in the boy. That this occurred to a musician, an artist who
deserved gratitude and admiration from life, adds an element of
deeper pathos and irony, as far as Lazarus was concerned.

Again, her blank verse is interesting and fresh. These are the
concluding lines of "Comoedia":

> The air was sweet with spring. On the third day,
> Amidst rejoicing thunder, the glad rush
> Of vivifying rains, and the white splendor
> Of unsheathed lightning, the aerial soul took flight,
> To mingle with its kindred elements.
> Applaud, my friends, the comedy is done.

Amid the tried and trite lyrics of this period, one poem, "Three
Friends" (*Lippincott's*, November 1879, pp. 615–16), displays partic-
ular virtuosity. Here are two sample stanzas:

> She was dead, the patient woman, tried by anguish
>   superhuman,
> Life had spent its worst on clean white flesh,
>   torn heart, thought-wearied brain;
> Death has so composed the features of this saddest
>   of Earth's creatures
> Not her deepest-stricken mourner dared have wished
>   her back again
>
>   .   .   .
>
> "Take thou comfort, O my brother," I made answer,
>   "Though none other
> May replace the large, sweet, tender soul this day
>   at last set free,
> Such a life leaves behind it, whereby one
>   may trace and find it,
> Like the moon's path on the waters, though the
>   moon has left the sea.

The basic meter is trochaic octameter, with variations that dispel the
tendency toward sing-song in such a meter. The first and third lines of

each stanza carry internal rhymes and these end on an unstressed syllable; the end-rhymed lines conclude with a stress, suddenly catalectic. Moreover, the internal rhyming (a device that drove even Poe to sounding like Ogden Nash once in a while) displays balance, control, and naturalness. Altogether, the poem delights by reason of the mixture of regularity and surprise. Better than Poe, Lazarus at this moment stands comparison with Browning.

II *Saint Ramauldo on His Deathbed*

The editors of *Lippincott's* in June 1873 gave six pages (663–68) to Emma Lazarus's dramatic monologue "Saint Ramauldo." Their decision was sound. Obviously influenced by the Browning manner of dramatic monologue, Lazarus pictures an old saint on his deathbed who recollects the crises of his life. All the hallmarks of the genre are here—setting, characterization, narrative—save one: there is no earthly listener; he is addressing the "saints of heaven."

The poem is in blank verse, and, as usual, Lazarus achieves in this form a realism and a flow only occasionally managed in her rhymed verse. The opening is dramatic in the technical sense; it serves as the exposition of place, character, and situation:

> I give God thanks that I, a lean old man,
> Wrinkled, infirm, and crippled with keen pains
> By austere penance and continuous toil,
> Now rest in spirit, and possess "the peace
> Which passeth understanding."
>
> (*Poems*, I, 130)

What he is thankful for is not the establishment of a "white society of snowy souls," but for the time and opportunity for his soul to have kept "severely rapt, her solitary course," despite "ignominy, malice, and affront."

A reminiscence of when he was "the wild lad" gives Lazarus the chance to write a beautiful quiet passage on nature that rings so much more true than dozens of descriptions of artificial Mays and Decembers:

> To stray alone among the shadowy glades,
> And gaze, as one who is not satisfied
> With gazing, at the large, bright, breathing sea,
> The forest glooms, and shifting gleams between
> The fine dark fringes of the fadeless trees. . . .
>
> (*Poems*, I, 132)

Immediately, the reminiscence turns to the time Ramauldo came upon the murder of his kinsman. Happening upon the scene, the youth had startled the murderer, who turns to him—it is the youth's father:

> The strange delusion wrought upon my soul
> That this had been enacted ages since.
> This very horror curdled at my heart,
> This net of trees spread round, these iron heavens,
> Were closing over me when I had stood,
> Unnumbered cycles back, and fronted *him*,
> My father. . . .

(Poems, I, 135)

The very rhetoric of the passage based on periods, parallels, and repetitions communicates brain-bursting horror.

The sequel to the youth's discovery is quickly told—how he hears the provident tolling of a monastery bell and escapes into this unworldliness and peace; how he condemns himself to loneliness and asceticism "to wrestle with my viewless enemies / Till they should leave their blessing on my head" (*Poems*, I, 138). And in time, like Jacob overcoming the Dark Angel, he succeeds. He remembers how he was driven out of the monastery and found peace as a hermit and later how he founded an order based on self-denial and saintliness. Now he is at the climax of a life of spiritual death and rebirth, satisfied with his suffering and end.

In characterization, this very competent dramatic monologue looks back to Browning. In tone, vocabulary, image, and even syntax, it anticipates the quiet narrative power of Edwin Arlington Robinson.

III   *Italian Melodrama*

The first we hear of *The Spagnoletto*, a three-act drama about the artist José de Ribera ("Il Spagnoletto"—the little Spaniard, 1591–1652) is in a letter from Ivan Turgenev to Emma Lazarus, October 23, 1876. He had not read the work yet, but remarked, "I don't doubt that I will find it worthy of the Author of 'Alide.' " [2] Let us hope that Turgenev was being kind, not sarcastic. Proof sheets were in Ralph Waldo Emerson's hands in November 1876, left there after Lazarus had read them to him during her August visit. [3] The quality and fate of this attempt at drama may be inferred from Emma's remark to Ellen Emerson in a letter of December 28: "I have given up all dreams of having my play produced on the stage—I am afraid it is not *act-*

able. . . ." [4] To say that it is not actable is not so bad: after all, her beloved Shelley, Byron, and Browning all wrote closet dramas. Hers, however, is nearly unreadable as well.

The drama tells of the Spagnoletto's intense hatred, because of past neglect, for the royalty for whom he paints portraits. He also harbors a possessive love of his daughter Maria. Secretly, Maria runs away with Duke John of Austria after his sojourn in Naples. Duke John betrays and leaves her. Ribera follows the couple, and in disguise as a monk visits the sorrowful, penitent, remorseful Maria. He then reveals himself, curses his daughter for the shame she has brought upon him, and, to ensure her everlasting pain of guilt, commits suicide in front of her. Here are all the dramatic elements that ever attracted Emma Lazarus—love, death, exotic people, fabulous settings. Moreover, the protagonist is an artist, and for him Lazarus tries to engender a special sympathy to offset his miserable nature and acts of enormity.

The sources to help her included Byron's enigmatic, possibly favorable comment, "Spagnoletto tainted / His brush with all the blood of the sainted" (*Don Juan*, XIII, stanza 71), as well as de Domenici's *Lives of the Painters, Sculptors, and Architects of Naples*, from which she took the apocryphal death of Ribera "uncritically" and "suppl[ied] the bloody catastrophe," complains Zeiger.[5] But such a complaint is no matter: a dramatist, as Shakespeare proved, is no historian nor meant to be. What is important is that Lazarus failed to motivate and integrate the two sides of Ribera's character.

All the characters in her play are set, posed, wooden, and unidimensional. The Spagnoletto leaps from extreme mood to extreme mood without realism or gradation. Maria is a melodramatic foil to him; Lorenzo, entirely the lovelorn swain; John, typically the smooth-talking, smirking sophisticate. That such simplicity of characterization can beguile a fluttering heart can be seen in Emma's sister Josephine's evaluation that the love scenes are "exquisitely tender and refined . . . the devoted girl with her heart in her eyes, on her lips, in her hand." Behind them, Josephine writes, hovers the Spagnoletto "like a tragic fate." [6] Not so, unfortunately: this is not tragedy, but the rankest melodrama. No one is heroic; no inevitable descent into catastrophe broods over the play; there is no catharsis of pity and terror. We sit only in wonder that Emma Lazarus, who did so well with the characterizations of several of her classical heroes and heroines, could not present here characters of subtlety, sympathy, and believability.

Josephine did identify the best that can be said of *The Spagnoletto*.
It does give us an amazingly immediate feeling of the Renaissance
atmosphere. In that sense it is a triumph of imagination.[7]

The poetry, blank verse patterned ultimately on Shakespeare by
way of Shelley and Browning, has the virtue of clarity, if not of fire and
imagery. Here is one of the better speeches:

> LORENZO   If my defect
> Be an hereditary grain i' the blood,
> Even as you say, I must abide by it;
> But if patrician habits more than birth
> Beget such faults, then may I dare to hope.
> Not mine, I knew, I felt, to clear new paths,
> To win new kingdoms; yet were I content
> With such achievement as a strenuous will,
> A firm endeavor, an unfaltering love,
> And an unwearying spirit might attain.
>
> *(Poems, I, 234)*

The Spagnoletto was never published; it was printed privately and
then reprinted in 1889 in her sisters' collection.

IV   *Thoughts Outside a Church*

In the light of the later "Jewish phase" of Lazarus's career, one
personal lyric of her middle period takes on some importance. "Outside the Church" was printed in the *Index* in December 1872. This
journal had been founded five years earlier by Theodore Parker, O.
B. Frothingham, and two of Lazarus's mentors, Thomas Wentworth
Higginson and Emerson. Its Transcendentalism was universalized by
the presence on its board of two religiously liberal rabbis, Isaac
Mayer Wise and Max Lilienthal.[8] Lazarus's poem answers the universalist tenor of the magazine.

Louis Ruchames, who researched the poem thoroughly, places its
composition "some time after her rejection of traditional Judaism and
prior to her whole-hearted acceptance of Transcendentalism."[9]
However, Emma was not reared so steeply in traditional Judaism that
there was much for her to reject at this time, and her espousal
of Transcendentalism is at least as old as her first book of poems, but
was never a doctrine to her—it was a name for a love of nature that her
master, Emerson, expounded on.

The Gothic church that either in imagination or in fact inspired the
poem represents first of all an object of art. She describes its "dark,

square belfry tower and massive walls" and its "oriel glass." Her response is initially sensitive to the hues that the sun casts through the mosaic, the tints, and the shadows, to the deep-voiced organ chords, the full-choired chant, and to the fine incense's sultry fragrancy. For a moment she is captured, together with those inside.

But only for a moment. She tried to yield to the embrace of "Mother-Church":

> I waited, but the message did not come
> No voice addressed my reason, and my heart
> Shrank to itself in chill discouragement.

In despair, she turns to Nature, and is answered:

> Estranged, unsatisfied, I issued forth
> (Not there again to look for peace and rest)
> Into the broad white light and large sweet air;
> And lo! the spring-tide beauty of the earth
> Touched tenderly the chord unreached, unguessed,
> And all my spirit melted in a prayer.
> . . .
> Here I stand, religion seems a part
> Of all the moving, teeming, sunlit earth;
> All things are sacred, in each bush a God. . . .

(p. 88)

Certainly, if this is serious, it is an extreme form of Transcendentalism, bordering on the impiety of Pantheism! Emerson never saw God in a bush, or in a cloud, like Pope's poor Indian. But Lazarus is not, despite Ruchames's assertion, "echo[ing] Emerson's dictum that 'Every natural fact is a symbol of some spiritual fact.' "[10] Emerson's Nature fed his spiritual certainty so that he could make such a pronouncement; Lazarus came to Nature by a process of elimination, if one were to believe "Outside the Church" as true autobiography. But, nonetheless, she does declare with Emerson, as Ruchames says, "the sacredness of all things," but only outside the church.[11]

This poem may well stand as a climax of Lazarus's career. It represents a sincere self-evaluation of her mind at the time she was writing lyrics for popular consumption, lyrics based on Nature, expressing universal thoughts. She could not know, of course, that in a few years new commitments engendering new images would intrude upon her, and that a higher achievement awaited her.

CHAPTER 6

Sonnets From Another Portuguese

FROM the day she wrote "Niagara," a blank-verse sonnet, in 1865, Emma Lazarus was fascinated by this genre. Between 1872 and 1881 she composed about fifty original and translated sonnets. She copied most of them into a manuscript notebook: many were published in various magazines, several had to wait until her sisters published them in the 1889 *Poems*, a few have not yet been published. Their themes ranged from love to current political events; that is, she tasted every theme that attracted sonneteers from Wyatt to Wordsworth. For her, it proved to be a very successful form.

I *Sonnets of Love*

Lazarus had long been writing odes and lyrics on love, innocuous professions of adoration as well as erotic fantasies. Now she turned to expressing these themes in the sonnet form. Two of them are set in the sea, a favorite locale that signals a plunge into innocent eroticism. "Phantasmagoria" was printed in *Lippincott's* in August 1876 and "Under the Sea," a two-sonnet poem, in the same magazine in October. Recalling the very first sea-poem she published, "The Sea Queen's Toilet," "Under the Sea" takes us into a new world, where

> Dark mosses clung,
> Golden and brown, to rocks that seemed fit couch
> For mermaidens and languid water-brides,
> Bright tawny bulging sea-weed in its pouch
> Held living jewels twinkling through the sides. . . .
> > (*Lippincott's*, October 1876, p. 476)

Laved by "the cradle-song of waves / And soft green waters kiss their sealed lips," she feels herself sinking beneath the water, but drowning seems to be a pleasant, be-kissed condition of sinking warmly into the liquid embrace of a lover's body.

Erotic dreaming will be found in sonnets in other settings, too, as in a manuscript sonnet called "Assurance." The entire text is given for two reasons: first, it is a typical example of Lazarus's use of her most frequent sonnet form, the Petrarchan; second, the setting and the imagery are, in her canon, startling:

ASSURANCE

Last night I slept, and when I woke her kiss
Still floated on my lips. For we had strayed
Together in my dream, through some dim glade,
Where the shy moonbeams scarce dared light
    our bliss.[1]
The air was dank with dew, between the trees,
The hidden glow-worms kindled and were spent.
Cheek pressed to cheek, the cool, the hot
    night-breeze
Mingled our hair, our breath, and came and went,
As sporting with our passion. Low and deep
Spake in mine ear her voice: "And didst thou dream,
This could be buried? This could be sleep?
And love be thrall to death! Nay, whatso seem,
Have faith, dear heart; *this is the thing that is!*"
Thereon I woke, and on my lips her kiss.

Zeiger thinks that this is "a lesbian fantasy, a variety of autism unique in her work" and therefore he warns against making too much of it psychoanalytically.[2] But why need the speaker of the poem be a woman? It would not be the first time that Lazarus presumed to speak the passion of a man. Nonetheless, Zeiger seems right in singling out "Assurance" for unusually explicit implications of erotic love. Statement ("sporting with our passion") is supported by striking, perhaps unconscious, images ("mingled . . . hair," glow-worms that "kindled and were spent"). It is no surprise that this poem was not published by Lazarus; the surprise is that she kept it, recopied it, and gave it a place in her fair manuscripts.

Usually, however, Lazarus keeps her virginal poise, as we see in a three-sonnet cycle on the stages of love, all under the title "Prothalamion." It was published in June 1877 in *Lippincott's*. Describing "First Love," Lazarus imagines a girl struck with new sensual responses to normal happenings, like seeing the twilight skies of early spring, smelling the fragrance of dew, and hearing the faint notes of birds. Strange feelings course through her body:

—dear God! What mean all these?
A strange aerial message subtly floats
From the Spring Spirit to the maiden's breast:
    She gazes forth with languid, dreamful eyes
On the expectant earth, the glowing West.
Upon her heart hath gained new unrest,
    The piercing thrill of some divine surprise,
    While one supreme star hold the boundless skies.

The next stage is called "Psyche," and reports the frenzied inner
urgings of the girl in love, desperately trying to fulfill her romantic
adage, "Who loves believes." She dreams, she wonders, she is in
torture, she is in bliss. But she contains all these emotions within—

            for she would not raise
The veil from those celestial mysteries,
Despite all taunts of envious tongues' despraise:
    Far rather quench the torch, smite blind her eyes
Than sacred love profane with worldly gaze.

When Lazarus reaches the ultimate stage of this love, "Marriage
Bells," nearly all the diction and fancy of archaic vocabulary fall away.
For this straightforward expression, she turns to the Shakespearean
form and writes her own sonnet on the marriage of true minds
without impediments:

MARRIAGE BELLS
Music and silver chimes and sunlit air,
    Freighted with the scent of honeyed orange-flower;
Glad, friendly festal faces everywhere.
    She, rapt from all in this unearthly hour,
With cloudlike, cast-back veil and faint-flushed cheek,
    In bridal beauty moves as in a trance
Alone with *him*, and fears to breathe, to speak,
    Lest the rare, subtle spell dissolve perchance.
But he upon that floral head looks down,
    Noting the misty eyes, the grave sweet brow—
Doubts if her bliss be perfect as his own,
    And dedicates anew with inward vow
His soul unto her service, to repay
Richly the sacrifice she yields this day.

                                                              (p. 707)

As a sonneteer on the theme of love, Emma Lazarus is nearly the
peer of no less a poet than Elizabeth Barrett Browning. A comparison

between them would be instructive, not so much to demonstrate influence, but to lament the obscurity of Emma Lazarus as a sonneteer in the history of the genre. Indeed, both poets started from the same premise, as one can see from these lines from the twenty-sixth of the *Sonnets from the Portuguese*:

> I lived with visions for my company,
> Instead of men and women, years ago,
> And found them gentle mates, nor thought to know
> A sweeter music than they played to me.

Two artistic women, two poets dependent upon dreams, both untouched by human passion, until one meets her man and the other is fated only to imagine that condition.

Here are two sonnets on a similar theme, one by Mrs. Browning, the other by Miss Lazarus. Both are so fine that identification of each with its author is difficult.

> Because thou hast the power and own'st the grace
> To look through and behind this mask of me
> (Against which years have beat thus blanchingly
> With their rains), and behold my soul's true face,
> The dim and weary witness of life's race!—
> Because thou hast the faith and love to see,
> Through the same soul's distracting lethargy,
> The patient angel waiting for a place
> In the new heavens!—because nor sin nor woe,
> Nor God's infliction, nor death's neighborhood,
> Nor all which others viewing, turn to go,
> Nor all which makes me tired of all, self-viewed,
> Nothing repels thee, Dearest, teach me so
> To pour out gratitude, as thou dost, good.

> What could I bring in dower? A restless heart,
> As eager, ardent, hungry, as his own,
> Face burned pale olive by our Southern sun,
> A mind long used to musings, grave, apart.
> Gold, noble name or fame I ne'er regret,
> Albeit all are lacking; but the glow
> Of Spring-like beauty, but the overflow
> Of simple, youthful joy. And yet—and yet—
> A proud voice whispers: Vain may be his quest,
> What fruit soe'er he pluck, what laurels green,
> Through all the world, for just this prize unseen

I in my deep heart harbor quite unguessed:
I alone know what full hands I should bring
Were I to lay my wealth before my king.

The first is the thirty-ninth of the *Sonnets from the Portuguese*; the
other, the second stanza of Lazarus's "Teresa di Faenza" (*Lippincott's*, July 1880, p. 83). It, too, is a valentine from a woman ready to
devote herself to her lover with admiration, gratitude, and selfless-
ness. Like Mrs. Browning, Lazarus restrains imagery, preferring a
direct, personal catharsis. Cast into modified Petrarchan mold,
"Teresa di Faenza" weds meter, rhyme, and structure to a vocabulary
that combines poetic quaintness with the colloquial without loss of
flavor, quite like Mrs. Browning's sonnet. It is lamentably unknown.

II *Sonnets from Music*

Between 1874 and 1881, Emma Lazarus composed a group of
sonnets inspired by the music of Robert Schumann and Frederic
Chopin. These poems are not only mood pieces occasioned by the
music or only posies to beloved composers; they also represent a
notion in Lazarus's mind that music is translatable into poems.

Her love of Schumann was demonstrated by a cycle of poems in
terza rima called "Phantasies," published in *Lippincott's* in August
1874. She was drawn to Schumann because of his attempts to fuse
ideas in literature and in music. He even derived inspiration from
precisely those poets Lazarus had been translating—Goethe,
Eichendorff, Heine, and even Byron. For Schumann, as for Emma
Lazarus, the introspective lyric was more congenial than the ballad.
In 1837, for example, Schumann composed *Phantasiestucke*, which
transposed literary moods into musical settings.[3] Lazarus merely
reversed the process back again. *Phantasies*, obviously inspired by
Schumann's cycle, has eight sections, the titles of which are translations of Schumann's titles of the movements of his composition.

The sentiments are similar to those she handled often. Melancholy, revery, the profundity of an evening's silence, languor, fancy,
are all rehearsed. Schumann's various moods evoke in Lazarus the
feeling of "fine influences" that fall at eventide and, like Shelley's
"intellectual beauty," at the same moment "suggest, foreshadow, or
recall [what] the spirit is alert to apprehend." Or they engender
feelings wherein, like Wordsworth and Tennyson—

> We can trust the faith which whispers prayer.
> The vanishings, the ecstasy, the gleam,
> The nameless aspiration, and the dream.
>
>   (*Poems*, I, 145)

Or they fashion a feeling that the world of dreams is a nightmare, representing a form of spiritual death, and the coming of morn symbolizes the usual spiritual rebirth.

Spiritual death and rebirth in a nature setting mark "Scenes in the Wood (Suggested by Robert Schumann)" (*Lippincott's*, August 1875, pp. 175–78). The cycle begins with a "Poem," followed by a "Hunting-Song." In part III, "Lovely Flowers," the mood descends from the joy and noise of the hunt to melancholy. There's a curious reference to Emerson here, perhaps to "The Rhodora," in the lines:

> Midst these [lovely flowers] my master's spirit
>   hovers near,
> The Northern singer, who hath led my feet
> To this enchanted ground.

In "Haunted Spot," the soul is terror-stricken by thoughts of evil, sin, insanity, and death. The upward turn comes as the soul alights upon a "Pleasant Prospect" and hears the "Bird as Prophet." Reminiscent of Keats and his nightingale, Lazarus cries to the bird:

> Whither may winged song follow you? where find
> The substance of those shades that cheat the mind?

Finally comes "Night," but the rejuvenation of the spirit is such that it overcomes the usual fears of night.

The peak of suggestiveness of Schumann's music upon Lazarus is the series of eight sonnets—Prelude, six fantasies, and an Epilogue—called "Symphonic Studies (After Robert Schumann)" (*Lippincott's*, November 1878, pp. 568–70). Music is a powerful, magical force in these poems. In "The Prelude" the composer is called Prospero, and all the connotations of the allusion to Shakespeare's *Tempest* are here—the power, the magic, the sea, the swelling of love, fairy voices, revery, and dream. The poet is victimized by the sound of music, a Miranda to Schumann's Prospero.

"Floating upon a swelling wave of sound/ We seemed to overlook an endless sea," and the music fashions in Lazarus's imagination

scenes beneath the sea. She imagines "audacious ventures of desire"—

> Oh, the wild voices of those chanting waves!
> The human faces glimpsed beneath the tide!
> Familiar eyes gazed from profound sea-caves,
> And we, exalted, were as we had died.
>
> *(Poems,* I, 207)

Here, as elsewhere in her poetry, "the sea was Life"—that is to say,
love, death, sexual sublimation. Schumann's music drowns her in this
nexus of ecstasy:

> Divided 'twixt the dream-world and the real,
> We heard the waxing passion of the song,
> Soar as to scale the heavens on pinions strong.
>
> *(Poems,* I, 210)

" 'Rage on, wild storm!' " the music seemed to sing to her, but the
passion is spent,

> The song was ended, and behold,
> A rainbow trembling on a sky of gold.
>
> *(Poems,* I, 210)

"Symphonic Studies" reiterates all the scenes and motifs of Lazarus's sea-poems since she had first essayed them in 1866, but what
must be noticed particularly here is the suppleness of her sonneteering. The sonnets of this sequence are Petrarchan in meter and rhyme
scheme. But the sense of abandon, of surrender to the pulsating
music, to the dream wish-fulfillments that swim subliminally, is
suggested by the reckless abandonment of structure in the first three
quatrains of each sonnet. Only the concluding couplets serve as
controls. Thus the passion of music begets passion in poetry, and the
intermixture sought by both Schumann and Lazarus is achieved.

The climax of this mixture of the arts is reached in the four sonnets
(three English, one Petrarchan) under the title "Chopin," published
in the *New York Times* on March 2, 1879. In two ways these sonnets
form a climax of this aspect of the Lazarus canon: first, Lazarus elides
entirely the separation between poet and composer; second, she can
find no solace in the music after it sends her down to despair.

Chopin was

> The Polish poet who sleeps silenced long,
> The seraph-souled musician, who breathes again
> Eternal eloquence, immortal pain.
>
> *(Poems, I, 204)*

From his "poetry" come "the entangling waltz," "the lyric prelude, the nocturnal song / Of love and languor." But all is not joy in his music:

> A voice was needed, sweet and true and fine
> As the sad spirit of the evening breeze,
> Throbbing with human passion, yet divine
> As the wild bird's untutored melodies.

Once again we are plunged into "sad reveries," but this time for Lazarus there is no recovery. Chopin was

> Rich gain for us! But with him is it well?
> The poet who must sound earth, heaven, and hell!
>
> *(Poems, I, 205–6)*

Music had touched the deepest responsive chord in Emma Lazarus. The artistic burden of music and poetry is precisely the same. And so are the divine and demonic rewards.

III   *Sonnets Occasional and Singular*

In moments of sudden self-evaluation, indeed, Lazarus seems to have doubted the relevance of her own poetry. "Late-born and woman-souled I dare not hope" is the striking first line that begins "Echoes," a manuscript sonnet dated October 10, 1880, unpublished until 1889.[4] "Late-born," she complains, means that "the freshness of the elder lays" is denied her; "woman-souled," she cannot express "manly modern passion." Therefore, instead of "twanging the full-stringed lyre through all its scope," she is limited. The sestet of the sonnet begs for the recognition of value in the kind of music that she is permitted, "elf-music."

Once or twice she tried to break away from the attraction of elf-music to confront the here and now. She wrote two sonnets under the title of "City Visions."[5] She is struck by "The glaring streets of brick and stone / Vexed with heat, noise and dust from morn till night." Yet she is inspired by "blind Milton's memory of light" and "dead Beethoven's phantasy of tone." So she, too, will

> . . . give rein to Fancy, taking flight
> From dismal now and here, and dwell alone
> With new-enfranchised senses.
>
> (*Poems*, I, 219)

Unable to take too much of this new setting, her senses soar "on wings of some rare poet's song," and she gains freedom, not from an assumed emotion, like sorrow, or from an imagined condition, like death; rather, the poet rises above an existential reality.

Lazarus even found current events congenial to sonneteering. She read about the death of the Prince Imperial, son of Napoleon III, in 1879 while he was an obscure officer in an obscure British regiment involved in an obscure battle in Africa. Immediately she saw in the incident possibilities of expressing favorite themes of the transiency of time and the irony of life. She penned two sonnets, "1856" (the year of his birth) and "1879" (the year of his death). Significantly, when reprinted in 1889, they were coupled under the heading "Destiny."

This child was "Heir to empire, to the purple born/ . . . one more Bonaparte." In the next two decades, however, his father lost his wars, his empire, and his homeland. Exiled to England with his wife and son, Napoleon III died in 1873. The prince became an officer in the British Army and there met his fate

> . . . lying stark and dead
> Transfixed with poisoned spears, beneath the sun
> Of brazen Africa.
>
> (*Poems*, I, 212–13)

She sees him as the victim of "follies and sins not thine." "Heartless howe'er [the world] be," it will pause to offer a dirge and to fling "rosemary and rue."

We might interpolate here, to complete the record, that she wrote longer poems on contemporary events that combine the current with the imagined. The assassination of Alexander II of Russia, March 13, 1881, gave vent to "Sic Semper Libertoribus" (*Century*, 27 [June 1881]), an angry attack upon those who nipped Russian liberation in the bud. The poem has a bit more significance as a prophesy of what she presently would say about Russia in essays on the anti-Jewish pogroms about to explode. The assassination of James A. Garfield, twentieth president of the United States, on September 19, 1881, occasioned "Sunrise" (*Critic*, October 8, 1881), an elegy that treated Garfield more kindly, heroically, and symbolically than history could.

Awareness of current affairs led Lazarus to thinking about economic class distinctions, an interest that was to prepare her for social work among the Russian-Jewish immigrants to New York later in the 1880s. Henry George was one of her mentors.

"After reading Mr. Henry George's book" in 1881, she wrote "Progress and Poverty," a sonnet in tribute, which George appreciated.[6] The sonnet reveals Emma Lazarus's socialistic leanings, derived, however, from a humanistic and not a doctrinaire base. This is an age of science, she declares, and humanity is sailing on an iron ship "to ports undreamed in history":

> . . . But where yawns the hold
> In that deep, reeking hell, what slaves be they
> Who feed the ravenous monster, pant and sweat,
> Nor know if overhead reigns night and day?

Though the shell of aristocratic gentility has cracked and Emma Lazarus is stepping gingerly into the world of reality, obeisance to the concept of the Artist naturally persists. As expressions of a personal commitment to Art, two sonnets deserve attention. Both deal with the image of birds as symbols of freedom of the poetic imagination.

The first is "The Cranes of Ibycus," dated, in the manuscript notebook, November 11, 1877. Its excellence was noted by E. C. Stedman, who published it in his collection of *Poets of America* in 1885, two years before Lazarus's death. It is nice to know that Stedman gave her a place in American literature that Emerson had denied her a decade before. The major image of the poem derives from a Greek legend about a poet who was attacked by robbers, and who as he died called to a flock of cranes to avenge his murder. Later, at a theatrical performance in Corinth, one robber saw cranes flying overhead and betrayed himself by crying out, "Lo the avengers of Ibycus!" [7] By some stream of connection, the cranes of Ibycus became to Lazarus symbolic of divine inspiration. For her persona—

> . . . Shadowy as a dream
> Was the prose-world, the river and the town.
> Wild joy possessed him; through enchanted skies
> He saw the cranes of Ibycus swoop down.
> He closed the page, he lifted up his eyes,
> Lo—a black line of birds in wavering thread
> Bore him the greetings of the deathless dead!

> (*Poems*, I, 214)

The other sonnet on the subject of poetic inspiration symbolizes the relationship of imagination to the gross world of actuality, again in the form of a bird:

THE TAMING OF THE FALCON

The bird sits spelled upon the lithe brown wrist
  Of yonder turbaned fowler, who had lamed
  No feather limb, but the winged spirit tamed
With his compelling eye. He need not trust
The silken coil, not set the thick-limed snare;
  He lures the wanderer with his steadfast gaze,
  It shrinks, it quails, it trembles yet obeys.
And, lo! he has enslaved the thing of air.
The fixed, insistent human will is lord
  Of all the earth;—but in the awful sky
  Reigns absolute, unreached by deed or word
    Above creation; through eternity,
  Outshining the sun's shield, the lightening's sword,
    The might of Allah's unaverted eye.[8]

There is no assumed sentiment of sorrow for the thing enslaved. Rather, Lazarus seems to have an exultant faith that moments of freedom will come, and indeed are more soaring, more powerful, and more victorious by reason of the contrast of these moments with the earth-bound life willed by the human being who knows no better. This sonnet is a sequel to "Links," the fine little poem in her first book about the soul's transcendent rise with the eagle and the lark. Now the falcon joins them. Perhaps the image of so strong a bird symbolizes Lazarus's growing self-confidence and self-regard as a poet as the decade of the 1870s ends.

CHAPTER 7

Excursions into Fiction

E MMA Lazarus wrote two works of fiction—a biographical novel,
Alide: An Episode of Goethe's Life, issued in 1874, and a story,
"The Eleventh Hour," published in 1878. In view of the new interest
in the theme of the Artist that she had been plying in her poetry, it is
significant that *Alide* is about a poet/dramatist and that the story is
about a painter.

I *Acolyte of Art*

From an essay, "Eugene Fromentin," that Lazarus wrote a bit later
(1881), we can surmise that she did not write *Alide* entirely with a
spontaneous overflow of storytelling intuition. She had a concept of
fictional form, structure, characterization, and tone by which she
judged Fromentin's only work of fiction, *Domenique* (he was an art
critic). This novel proved to be congenial to Lazarus, for like *Alide*,
Domenique deals with what Lazarus called "a forbidden passion" and
the "motif of the story [she opines] presents nothing new." What is
much more important "is the originality of types, the picturesque of
scene, the sincerity of accent, the trenchant or eloquent passages of
reflection and criticism, the wonderful grace and tenderness of touch,
that the peculiar charm of the book consists." [1] This Lazarus had
striven to put into her own novel of a forbidden passion.

Fromentin's heroine, Madeline, "is a highly poetic figure, but
somewhat unreal and over-idealized," wrote Lazarus, in an accurate
judgment about her own heroine, Alide. The hero of *Domenique* (like
the one in *Alide*) is a "nervous, sentimental, poetical youth" who
ignores the "counsels of wise friend[s]." Echoing the judgments of
reviewers of *Alide*, Lazarus finds *Domenique* "very human, very
melancholy, and singularly beautiful . . . , concluded in a natural
frame *of serenity*, silence, and regret" [her italics].[2]

Thus we perceive a kind of theory of fiction. Originality is to be
looked for not in plot but in execution. The beauty of a piece of fiction

is fashioned by purity of technique, moral sentiment, and tastefulness of characterization. The secret didacticism of the conclusion—since melancholy and regret often accompany a moral decision—epitomizes the heroism. Altogether it is artistry achieved by denial of the flesh and blood.

For her first attempt at fiction, Lazarus turned to a favorite poet's life. The source of *Alide* is John Oxenford's translation of *The Autobiography of Goethe. Truth and Poetry From My Own Life*, books X–XI.[3] Goethe describes there his brief, idyllic relationship with Fredricka Brion, and Lazarus reworks the incident with several changes of plot, but with general fidelity. One reviewer wrote, "There was great risk in taking for a theme a love-passage in the life of a renowned poet—one, too, which had been faultlessly treated by himself in his autobiography," but Lazarus avoids the pitfalls of too much invention and of "any ambitious attempt to penetrate deeply into Goethe's character."[4]

Striving for the novelist's conventional omniscience, Lazarus assumes a superior, sophisticated pose that sounds far more experienced than the twenty-five years at which she wrote the book. She describes Julius Steck (Goethe's alias at this point in the plot) as viewing the countryside where he will encounter Alide "with the eyes of an artist rather than of a boy just turned twenty." For him and his friend Max Waldstein, the landscape serves "to overpower with quieting suggestions even the exuberant buoyancy of spirits natural to their age." But Emma is not so omniscient as to avoid the startling suggestiveness (never elaborated upon, of course) of her analogy of the relationship of Max to Julius to that of "a girl to the magnetic, myriad-sided nature of his fellow-lodger, the boy-artist."[5]

Picturesqueness of scene may be exemplified by Lazarus's description of the parsonage in which Alide lives. It is like a picture postcard of a quaint Rhenish scene. It is antique, weatherbeaten, and ivy-covered, lifting its "humble spire" into the "mellow warmth" of the October light. A "small, carefully-tended garden" borders it, in which a "perky little hen, with her brood close by," hops (18–19). Inside, a homey disorder charmed the sudden guests. *Lippincott's* reviewer, however, with a surprising desire for Realism, criticized this passage as "more like that of an English than a Rhenish home" because it lacked Teutonic primness and order, but concluded that Lazarus's description is "very pretty" nevertheless.[6] It is also a compliment to Lazarus's imagination, for she had not yet visited either scene.

Lazarus's narrative technique in this novel depends heavily on ironic foreshadowing. For example, soon after the boys are invited into this pretty little parsonage, Alide sings an Alsatian love song that affects young Goethe to tears as an indication of things to come in their relationship (37). Then Lazarus immediately interpolates a heavy-handed preview of the revelation of Steck's real identity by having Waldstein say, "Wolfgang Goethe! . . . Of course I know him;—All Strasbourg knows him already. . . . He is only a jovial fellow like the rest of us" (38). And a bit later, Waldstein berates his friend for attempting "to examine these pastoral, idyllic lives with entire freedom from personal emotions" (47). Little does Waldstein know how soon personal emotions will blot out Goethe's intellectual coolness!

The first object of his love is not Alide. Her sister Rahel first attracts Goethe: however, in a series of clichés, Alide, in the "perfect flowering of maidenhood," falls in love with him as the "dewy light of the young day" wanes (58,52). That night a storm, conveniently symbolic of the storm within her, breaks: "The simple girl clasped her hands together, and, kneeling by her bedside, implored the blessing and protection of Heaven upon this stranger so suddenly endeared to her" (79). The point of this irony is of course that Goethe not only falls, but falls for the child Alide in a triumph of personal emotions.

The major conflict involves an impossible love, a conflict that demands the woman's sacrifice, a normal plot in lesser but vastly popular Victorian fiction. Characterization is one stratum above superficiality. Action is staged, it does not occur. The creation and manipulation of dramatic foils are obvious and predictable—Goethe's mercurial artistic temperament is set off by Waldstein's earthy good nature; Alide's stereotyped innocence and demeanor are contrasted with the suave, worldly-wise gracefulness of her cousin Anna Burckhardt and with the passion of Lucinda, Goethe's former love. People talk as if their grammar teachers wrote the dialogue: Goethe has just kissed Alide and she whispers, "I love you," to which Goethe replies, "Rise, my beloved; we will take a walk through the meadows; the fresh air will cool your flushed cheeks, and we shall be able to meet once more with composure our friends" (115). A modern reader may wonder how any girl could warm to such a character.

The sharpest point of plot in the novel concerns the curse levelled by Goethe's previous paramour, Lucinda, upon "her who kisses these lips for the first time after me" (99). In the *Autobiography* this is merely an innocent remark by the daughter of a dancing teacher,[7] but

Lazarus seizes upon it as the controlling ironic device in the last part of her novel. In the development of this line of narrative architecture, she shows herself best as a fiction writer. The curse is first reported to Alide by Goethe himself as they stand together in the Cathedral. Then he remorsefully recalls the curse in a dream (120). The climax of this motif occurs appropriately back in the Cathedral, when Alide sees a woman, dressed in black, faint away, and rushes to help her. In French, the woman calls Alide an angel. Alide asks, "Your name?" "Lucinda." Chapter finis (173). And ultimately, as the last phase of the irony, the curse comes to pass. Alide breaks with Goethe, he to climb the heights of fame, she to remain celibate and lonely in unrequited love.

There are only heroes and heroines in *Alide*, no villains, no despicable characters. Goethe is depicted as a gay young poet as well as an egotistical lover in his treatment of Alide. But Lazarus's defense is clear: he is an Artist, and an Artist has a duty beyond the ken of simple innocent country girls. Lazarus offers this defense in a scene which has Goethe reading *Hamlet* to Alide and his sophisticated friends. Goethe remarks to the group that Hamlet "sincerely loved [Ophelia]—before the play. . . . But from the moment that his capacities are disclosed to him . . . he is bound by the highest duty of man—that which he owes himself—to discard everything that can cramp or impede the development of his own nature. . . . He simply outgrows her" (153).

As for the characterization of the heroine, Alide emerges from the initial unidimensional girlish innocence in the country into a woman of greater resilience and understanding in the city with Goethe. There is a touch of irony here, because Goethe sees Alide as bereft of "poetry" when she is transplanted from the countryside into the company of sophisticated city cousins. Yet it is in this alien environment that she develops depth. Alide's decision to break off with Goethe is contained in a speech of idealistic sacrifice: "You, dear friend, will advance on a brilliant, an unexampled career; but if I be drawn from my proper element I shall suffocate and die. . . . If I cannot say, wherever you go, I will follow, . . . if I cannot say that, I know that I have no right to call myself your wife" (188). However, in a touch of realistic characterization unique in the novel, Lazarus has her write to Goethe later that this was a lie: "A word, a gesture, a simple impulse of the old tenderness, would have brought me to your side again, and made me deny every word I had that minute spoken" (203). With this, the novel reaches its effective conclusion.

Nearly all the reviewers liked it. The *Boston Advertiser* said that "Miss Lazarus has the strength, grace and simplicity of style, and treats with equal skill both the outer and inner life of his character." [8] Less sanguine, *Lippincott's* review criticized style and elements of technique, but still found the character of Alide "not a copy but a development of that of Fredrika," and "the human interest is keenly felt . . .[in] the power and truth in the analysis of the conflict." [9] The reviewer in the *Jewish Messenger* sensed the theme of the conflict of the Artist and, with a twist of irony, cast Emma Lazarus in the role of a putative Alide; "Miss Lazarus is to be praised for her devotion to art, which prompts her to subordinate a natural ambition [to create a new character] to the true chivalry of a faithful servant of Goethe." [10]

The most surprising critical comment on *Alide* came from the pen of Ivan Turgenev. Lazarus had sent him a copy of the book together with a graceful note about how deep an impression his novel of Russian nihilism, *Virgin Soil*, made upon her. [11] Turgenev's reply is amazing. His ecstasy can be explained only by his gallantry. First, he says she overcame his feeling that "celebrated modern men—especially poets and artists"—are not good subjects for fiction. Then he tells her he found *Alide* "very sincere and very poetical," and the "characters are drawn with a pencil as delicate as it is strong." He appreciates her expression of his influence upon her, but, he concludes, "an author who writes as you do—is not a 'pupil in art' anymore, [but is close to being] a master." [12]

On the other side, the *New York Commercial Advertiser* (April 10, 1874), though it found Lazarus "original" in the sense of "subtlety or exhibition of peculiar fragments of truth," and writing with "a certain clearness, freshness, and sanity of perception," nevertheless places the book in proper perspective: "A work of this kind is necessarily slight [because the author is] not ready to trust [her]self to [her] own power of invention," depending as she does on the life and work of another author. This is kindness judicially balanced, which is the best that can be done with *Alide*.

II   *The Artist Rescued*

Lazarus's story of an impoverished artist in an uncultured society was published four years later. For Arthur Zeiger, "The Eleventh Hour" "duplicate[s] hackneyed products of countless formula-bound fictioneers." [13] Sergius Azoff, "penniless and friendless," becomes the lion of a group of rich New York women as "the most gifted young painter in town." They support him by becoming his pupils. Azoff makes the acquaintance of Ellen and Richard (Dick) Bayard, and Sergius becomes Ellen's special interest. She gives him entrée into her household, but Dick, after tolerating his presence for a time, orders the relationship broken. Dick calls Azoff a "fawn." After a brief disobedience, Ellen becomes frightened of "arous[ing] the passions of such a man," who is of Eastern origin, artistic, and with a "sylvan, untamed naturalism."

The story now shifts from Ellen and Sergius to Dick and Sergius. Dick learns that the artist is an opium-eater who is going down, down, down. He meets him working on a road gang in Central Park. This changes Dick's attitude: Sergius becomes "the bravest and noblest man [he] ever met." Dick listens to his sad tale of illegitimate birth, social alienation in Europe, and artistic alienation in the American environment. In fact, Sergius had just written a suicide note. At the eleventh hour, Dick has saved him! "And in the gray light of the morning which broke in like a promise and encouragement, the stately artist in his mean attire and the loyal-eyed American stood and clasped each other's hands." [14]

Yet some good things might be said. The picture of New York society mesdames fawning on the young artist comes across with a realism and bite that betrays a touch of Jamesian social observation. "Never before had so many of the wealthiest merchants' and bankers' daughters been inspired with a zealous devotion to Art. . ." (242). Lazarus's characterization of Ellen Bayard, bored but adventuresome, is realistic and admirably complex. Ellen "was an arch-woman, simple and cunning, vain and disinterested, noble and petty, capable of entering with ardent enthusiasm into the thoughts and feelings of others, yet always retaining in the fervor of her generous emotion an undefined pleasant consciousness of her own sympathetic qualities" (244). Ellen's sympathy for Sergius is tempered by "her feel[ing] all through the day a complacent sort of pleasure, a subdued, triumphant sense of power, in imagining his unhappiness" (245).

Echoes from Henry James, a fellow contributor to the *Century* in these years, may be detected also in the themes of the artist fighting for his artistic life and the culture of Europe versus the philistinism of America. Of course, that's as far as a comparison can go. James would never have permitted himself the treacly sentiment and childish climax to the tale. It is well that after "The Eleventh Hour" Lazarus left off writing fiction. Josephine Lazarus retorts that Emma, in the last years of her life, began a novel, but illness forced her to abandon it.[15] The few chapters she wrote are not extant, but then—to judge from the two pieces of fiction she did write—this is not to be lamented. Fiction was not her metier.

CHAPTER 8

Excursions into Criticism

FROM essays, reviews of dramatic and musical performances, letters, and even poems, emerges the critical thought of Emma Lazarus. The operative criteria for her critical approaches derive from a passage in "The Poet" (1841, 1844) by her erstwhile master, Ralph Waldo Emerson:

> We have yet had no genius in America, with tyrannous eye, which knew the values of our incomparable materials, and saw, in the barbarism and material-ism of the times, another carnival of the same gods whose pictures he so much admires in Homer. . . . Our log-rolling, our stumps and their politics, our fisheries, our Negroes and Indians, our boats and our repudiations, . . . the northern trade, the southern planting, the western clearing, Oregon and Texas, are yet unsung. Yet America is a poem in our eyes; its ample geogra-phy dazzles the imagination, and it will not wait long for meters.[1]

Independence, realism, and vision—these are the keynotes sounded in this passage. Emma Lazarus displays understanding of their im-port more clearly in her criticism than in her practice of poetry.

I *On Our Literature*

A poem she included in *Admetus and Other Poems* entitled "How Long?" is an analogue of these passages from "The Poet." It, too, is a sort of declaration of poetic independence from England. "That distant isle," she cries, ". . . too long hath been our mistress and our queen." With naive, ingenuous irony, she complains, "Too late, too late we cling/To alien legends, and their strains prolong"—this, in a book where she devotes more than half the number of pages to these various alien legends. Nonetheless, she proudly declares with Emerson:

> This fresh young world I see,
> With heroes, cities, legends of her own;

> With a race of men, and overblown
>   By winds from sea to sea,
> Decked with the majesty of every zone.
>
>   *(Poems,* I, 54)

Though the vision is apt, Lazarus was first among those who could not take advantage of such incomparable materials.

She expressed a similar view of American literary history in a letter written to E. C. Stedman in the summer of 1881. In a gesture of highest respect, Stedman had sent to her for her criticism the first chapter of *Poets of America* which he had prepared for publication as an article for *Century.*[2] Her reply is a prose elaboration of the poem "How Long?" She is still calling for the poet who will creep out from under the European cultural blanket and fare forth to find his themes in America.

Lazarus could not agree with Stedman that "adverse conditions" and lack of culture accounted for the absence of the great American poet. Themes always existed for "clear-eyed seers" like Dante, Shakespeare, and Milton. And before Burns and Scott no one had found "romance & melody" in the "rich *patois* of the grim old Highlander & barbarous music of the bagpipes." Yet they existed, waiting for recognition. She writes further:

I never believed in the *want of a theme*—wherever there is humanity, there is the theme for a great poem—& I think it is the poet's fault if he do not know how to utilize the accessories & materials which surround him. All you say is wise, keen, & absolutely true of American poetry—but if the Genius had been born, I cannot help believing all these objections & impediments would have been blown to the winds with the first sweep of his lyre.[3]

Yet she is ambivalently capable of defending American literature. In an essay entitled "American Literature,"[4] she attacks George Woodberry's thesis that American literature has no tradition ensuing from Irving, Hawthorne, Longfellow, and Emerson. "All men of genius are isolated, even from their followers," Lazarus declares, and she identifies as her example Ralph Waldo Emerson: "Whoever fails to see in Emerson's work the flowering of a distinctive American school of thought and habit, fails to understand the essential spirit of his teaching." Indeed, not only has Emerson found followers in Thoreau, Burroughs, and the current stars, Lowell, Henry James senior, Stedman, Stoddard, and Howells, but in England as well. She quotes Carlyle's "hackneyed sentence": " 'I hear many echoes, but only one voice—from Concord.' "

On another point: Woodberry had asserted that except for the accident of Hawthorne's birth, *The Marble Faun* is as much English as American. To which Lazarus replied that, by this criterion, George Eliot's *Romola* is as much Italian as English, except that Eliot was born English. "In each case," Lazarus concludes, "we consistently exclude the essentially national and even more powerful works of the same author . . . [like Hawthorne's] 'Scarlet Letter.' " [5]

And yet again, a persistent disappointment in the current state of American literature is hinted in a manuscript poem entitled "The Old Year—1883." Lazarus begs for a reversion of Time to live once again in greater days—and recounts only the glories of *British* poets as exemplars of great literature. So, as late as 1883, as far as Emma Lazarus is concerned, the American Genius seems not yet to have been born.

II   *The Ways of a Poet*

In several earlier lyrics, Lazarus had described the world of poetry and expounded upon the poet's divinity. Now she undertakes to examine the ways of the poet. A sonnet, "Life and Art" (dated in manuscript December 1882), is a restatement, in perfect Petrarchan form, of Wordsworth's famous sentence about what poetry is. Lazarus's poet is pictured "while the fever of the blood is strong, / The heart throbs loud," but not then "the Nurse shall bless / The Poet-soul to help and sooth with song." Only "when the dream is done, the pulses fail, / The day's illusion, with day's sun set"—in other words, when the original spontaneous overflow of powerful feelings is recollected in tranquility—then the "divine Consoler," will

> Enter and clasp his hand and kiss his brow.
> Then his lips ope to sing—as mine do now.
>
> > (*Poems*, I, 217)

Keats was apparently in her mind when she wrote "Critic and Poet: An Apologue" (dated January 1884). The "critic" is called here a "naturalist," he of the analytical mind, who studies and defines "*what is a bird.*" The critic is busy with classification of genre and notation of the song—"when of a sudden,—hark, the nightingale." The critic sees only "the plain brown warbler," not the bird who produced a song "deeper, higher than he could divine." Because the nightingale does not answer to his law, he declares, "No bird is this" (*Poems*, I, 215). This is a poet's perennial complaint against the critic, who, as usual, is pictured as so barnacled by ancient rules of rhetoric and genre that he cannot appreciate the flights of a poet's fancy. However, the attack on the critic is unworthy of Lazarus. In the first place, she rarely strayed off the beaten methods of versifying tried-and-true subjects, and so never invited censure for taking flight; in the second place, the critics liked her poetry as it was.

Her traditionalism is emphasized in a review of a musical performance by one Rafael Joseffy in New York in October 1879. The year 1879 is the eve of her translating Heine after years of briefer excursions into translation. It is significant, therefore, that she sees Joseffy as a translator of other men's genius. When Joseffy played Beethoven she liked him because he imparted "just enough of his own subjectivity . . . to bestow the requisite color and warmth." She did not like his rendition of Liszt's "Hungarian Rhapsody No. 2" because "there were too many innovations and unwarrantable liberties taken with the score." [6] Now Lazarus turns to consider originality in poetry:

We are apt to demand, over and above all mechanical gifts, the presence of an original individuality. There must be the subtle poetic spirit, which, while disdaining all sensational effects, deals in constant surprises of beauty or power, keeping the mind of the listener ever on the alert, in a truly intellectual enjoyment, the heart in a strange glow, beating with unwonted excitement, sonorous with the vibrations of chords unguessed, long silent, but instantaneously responsive to the master-touch. [7]

This is a vision of her ideal poem, the poem she perhaps thought she wrote, the will-o'-the-poetic-wisp she chased, but only occasionally approached.

III   *Lazarus and the "-isms"*

Lazarus was not unaware of the storms which had arisen in France concerning the "-isms" of critical theory—specifically, in her day, Classicism, Romanticism, and Realism.

As might be expected, in view of the first cultural sources of inspiration in her poetic life, she initially identified Classicism with reality. She showed indignant impatience with critics who placed Classicism in a world apart from life and nature. One of those critics was J. A. Symonds, whose *Sketches and Studies in Southern Europe* she reviewed in 1880. She attacks Symonds for pitting "Greek love of beauty, light and art . . . [,] the outward pomp and bravery of nature," against the reality of "inward agonies and martyrdom of man."

She ridicules Symonds's judgment that once one has "stepped suddenly . . . from Greek legends of the past to the real Christian present, . . . nothing can identify [him] with the simple, natural earth." [8] To Lazarus, Greek legends, Nature, simplicity of life, and life's pains are all part of one experience.

Indeed, Classicism as the ballast for unworldliness is a motif of "Ariel and Euphorion," an elegy on the deaths of Shelley and Byron.[9] Shelley is Ariel, a pure sprite as in *The Tempest*. Lazarus's descriptions of his songs are reminiscent of Poe's ethereal poet, Israfel, for Ariel, too, is capable of "celestial strains," "spheral melody," "realms ethereal." Altogether, however, his poems are beautiful but insubstantial. On the other hand, Byron is Euphorion, the offspring of Faust and Helena, "born of the union of the Romantic and the Classic," Lazarus tells us in a headnote. Because Euphorion has his feet grounded in reality, he is not enervated by Ariel's death. He continues to "live, love, and sing." The combination of the idealism of Romanticism and the realism of Classicism in Euphorion's poetry prevailed.

Byron reappears as Phaon in a long manuscript poem of that name. In Greek myth, Phaon was a beautiful youth who was the cause of Sappho's suicide; why Lazarus chose him as the representative Romantico-Classical poet is not clear. In her poem, Phaon is a poet on a spiritual journey searching for cosmic certainty. Denied revelation, he resigns himself to be a poet for humanity, striving in his limited sphere to express a perception of beauty by means of his "light serene."

Thus far, Lazarus has distinguished between Romanticism as the expression of an ethereal world and Classicism as the expression of the real world. She has seen no reason to place them in opposition to each other; rather, her view is that they complement each other. Now, however, her critical position is complicated by the importation from France of a new critical term, Realism.

Gordon S. Haight tells us what this new concept meant in the era of Lazarus:

As early as 1826, the word *réalisme* was used in France to describe a literary method that attempted faithful imitation of originals found in nature; it was contrasted, not with romanticism, but with classicism, which tended toward the imitation of art rather than nature. Both the romanticist and realist tried to give detailed transcripts of the world about them.[10]

Undismayed by this new program of critical terms, Lazarus assimilated the new critical terminology into her system in a review of a dramatic performance, "Bernay as 'Mark Antony,'" in 1883:

[Bernay's] art belongs to the romantic, realistic school, as opposed to the classic and antique. I use, advisedly, the apparently contradictory terms "romantic" and "realistic" for the great romantic revival initiated in literature by Rousseau and his followers, and developed by Goethe, Byron, Scott, and all the poets of the eighteenth century, was but the protest of truth, nature, and realism, against cant in morals and the artificial in art. By the singular effect of a violent reaction, romanticism today in its turn has come to signify the very antithesis of truth and reality. But this interpretation is only a passing accident resulting from the extreme point to which the movement was carried, and does not alter the fact that the best art may be at the same time very romantic and very real.[11]

These thoughts are harbingers of modern criticism, wherein the term Realism has taken over the optimistic cast once attributed to Romanticism, and a new term, Naturalism, is used to name the mode of expressing pessimism. Anticipating this development of critical terminology, Lazarus reinterpreted her beloved Classicism as outmoded and unworldly, redolent of cant and artificiality. Clearly, her shift in criticism reflects the shift in the nature of her poetry. By 1883, she had entered her Jewish phase, and an unadorned confrontation with reality was the cause. Never again was there a place in her poetry for the surface glitter of "Classicism."

IV *Tribute to William Morris*

Lazarus's concept of the Poet and the inspiration of Realism was one of the motivations for her pilgrimage in 1883 to visit William Morris. On July 6 of that year, during her tour of England, she arranged to meet Morris in his famous factory. She came to him with some experience in socialistic communal undertakings on behalf of Russian Jewish refugees in New York, and Morris was the prime exemplar of the combination of art and social responsibility in the real world.

To Lazarus, William Morris was a British Walt Whitman, with whom she compares him. He "is a poet made manifest in the fine modeling and luminous expression of the features," endowed with a "well-equipped and powerful individuality." Morris, too, achieved in his poetry "that virginal quality of springtide freshness and directness which we generally miss in modern literature, and which belonged to Chaucer and Homer."[12]

His artistic temperament manifested itself in his benign and enlightened business approach. Morris represented the successful confluence of cause and word, art and agitation, poet and personality,

Romanticism and Realism. No doubt she was thinking also of herself when she wrote of Morris that "no thwarted ambitions, no stunted capacities, no narrow, sordid aims have ranged him on the side of the disaffected, the agitator, the outcast," [13] only an altruistic humanism.

More than anything else, perhaps, Morris sanctified her own plunge into the sordid world of wretched refugees. She confirmed, that day in Surrey with William Morris, that Realism and a social consciousness are no obstacles to poetry.

CHAPTER 9

Homage to Heine

E MMA Lazarus had revealed her regard for Heinrich Heine's poetry in 1866, when she published translations of fifteen of his lyrics in her first book of poems. Over the ensuing years, however, Heine (1797–1856) took second place first to Hugo and then to Goethe. But he was never forgotten: she closed *Admetus* with one of his songs and contributed two translations to *Lippincott's* in 1876. Finally, his turn came in 1881 in a book of translations entitled *Heinrich Heine: Poems and Ballads.*[1] The importance of this book in the life and work of Lazarus lies not merely in the translations, but even more in the Introduction she wrote and the followup essay she published a few years later.

I *Dreams, Death, the Grave*

What was Heine's attraction for Emma Lazarus so that, during a lifetime of translating, she was moved to compile a full book from his work? At first, his sentimental brand of Romanticism called to her heart. In fact, Geraldine Rosenfeld, who studied their relationship most deeply, claims that Schumann's musical settings of some of Heine's verses inspired Lazarus to translate him.[2] Lazarus's interest in Schumann makes this plausible, but only ancillary to an ongoing response since the 1860s to Heine's decadent Romanticism. Lazarus selected for translation for her book mainly several cycles of early poems that were not really representative of Heine's work because they expressed themes, as Frederick Ewen said, of "dreams, death, the grave, the supernatural, all the faded paraphernalia of a dying romanticism,"[3] —precisely those themes that dominated her own work until 1880. Thus, H. B. Sachs should not have been so struck as to write, "Very curious is the link between that bitter, mocking, cynical spirit and the refined, gentle spirit of Emma Lazarus."[4] She ignored those poems that betrayed his bitterness and cynicism. Moreover, the pure aesthetism in Heine's work appealed to her—

"the magic of his verse, the irridescent play of his fancy," said Josephine Lazarus.[5] The Greek love of beauty for its own sake, the playing with paganism, the worship of the Classical paralleled Lazarus's early interests. Aaron Kramer sums up the connection: "Heine, more than any other guide outside of Emerson, was her spiritual and aesthetic guide." [6]

A few examples will suffice to illustrate the type of lyric that attracted Lazarus. From Heine's "Early Poems" she translated "The Vale of Tears" (in 1872 or thereabouts Lazarus wrote her own poem based on this biblical allusion), a short narrative of two lovers, emaciated unto death. When the coroner and the "worthy leech" find them, they opine that in "nippy weather" one should have wholesome food and flannels to wear (*Heine*, p. 65). In "Solomon," the king dreams of his beloved:

> O Shulamite, the lord of all these lands am I,
>   This empire is the heritage I bring,
>   For I am Judah's king and Israel's king,
> But if thou love me not, I languish and I die.
>
> (*Heine*, p. 66)

Such an exotic and sophomoric note is heard in her poetry, too.

In a cycle entitled "Homeward Bound," dedicated by Heine to Frederika Vanhagen von Ense, Emma Lazarus found forms and themes that she had been plying for years. Here is a typical stanza:

> In my life, too full of shadows,
>   Beamed a lovely vision bright.
> Now the lovely vision's vanished,
>   I am girt about by night.

Indeed, Heine's imagery flows from the same sources as Lazarus's and is given a similar cast, as we see in his use of the metaphor of the seasons:

> My heart, my heart is heavy
> Though merrily glows the May
> Out on the ancient bastion
> Under the lindens, I stay.
>
> Heart, my heart, oh, be not shaken!
> Bravely bear thy fate. Once more

> Shall the coming Spring restore
> What the Winter rude hath taken.

We should have expected Emma Lazarus to think this laudable poetry when Heine wrote such sentimental stuff in the style and form of a gifted juvenile. "I hope you will be pleased with my efforts at reading Heine," she wrote to Rabbi Gustav Gottheil on June 29, 1881. "You must not think of him as you know him [Gottheil had come from Germany], but of the English-speaking people to whom he is a dead letter." [7] She knew what the American public wanted—simplicity and sentiment. This she gave them in her own and Heine's work.

II   *"Tannhäuser" Again*

Only the coincidence that Lazarus wrote a version of the Tannhäuser legend for *Admetus and Other Poems* a decade before causes us to glance at this translated rendition of the story. Of course, certain narrative elements are the same: Tannhäuser, a knight, falls into the clutches of a lustful Venus, rejects her, is exiled, and flees to Rome to ask the Pope's pardon, only to be refused. Beyond this no connection exists. Heine has Tannhäuser wander back to Venusberg. In Lazarus's treatment, Tannhäuser is a bard, and wanders in continual search for absolution. Nor did Lazarus lighten her telling with the touches of cynical humor that Heine did. For example, when Tannhäuser returns, Heine's Venus embraces him so heartily that her nose bleeds. Then

> The Knight lay down upon her bed,
>   And not a word he spake,
> Dame Venus to the kitchen went
>   A bowl of broth to make.

> (p. 53)

Of this playfulness Lazarus was incapable.

Doggedly, she goes on for a while, translating what seems to have been Heine's major purpose in his version: a bitter comment on the state of contemporary German literary and public politics. Tannhäuser commences to tell Venus about his journey to Rome and back through Europe. In Germany, "The people are crying Goethe's dead, / And Eckermann's still alive!" and no word of Heinrich Heine, who saw himself, Lazarus tells us in the Introduction (pp. 20–21), as next in line to Goethe, " 'my colleague No. 1 . . . Grand Ducal Weimarian Jupiter.' " At this point, Lazarus breaks off her transla-

tion, noting that she did not finish the eight more verses to this poem
(*Heine*, p. 55). She did not translate, Aaron Kramer writes, a series of
impish, satirical, vitriolic stanzas, and "the modern reader . . . is
likely to find her little piece of censorship more shocking than even
those eight stanzas of vitriol could be." [8] But the modern reader is
just as likely to prefer Lazarus's melodramatic Tannhäuser to Heine's
cynical, personal animus.

III   *A Dose of Jewish Irony*

Lazarus's most interesting renditions in the *Poems and Ballads* of
Heine involve a ballad called "Donna Clara," from *Die Heimkehr*
(1824). To speak first of technical matters, we note that the meter is
trochaic pentameter in a quatrain stanza; the poem does not rhyme,
either in German or in English, but cantering along on its trochaics
the ballad does not miss rhyme. Heine's use of incremental repetition
and parallelism serves not only to augment the bardic tone of the
ballad, but also to sharpen ironies; to this quality Lazarus was
attuned.

The plot is based on love and a twist of irony, in conventional ballad
fashion. Donna Clara, the Alcalde's daughter, is smitten with a
mysterious suitor who nightly calls to her on his zither. One night,
during a ball, while walking through her garden, Donna Clara is
suddenly confronted by "the handsome knightly stranger." Then
ensues a form of conventional question-and-answer sequence that
brings a new and startling element into the plot, anti-Semitism
during the Inquisition:

The knight whispers to her in their passionate embrace:

> "Tell me, tell me, my beloved,
>   Wherefore all at once thou blushest?"
>
> "Gnats were stinging me, my darling,
>   And I hate these gnats in summer,
> E'en as though they were a rabble
>   Of vile Jews with long, hooked noses."
>
> "Heed not gnats or Jews beloved,"
>   Spake the knight with fond endearments.
> From the almond-trees dropped downward
>   Myriad snowy flakes of blossoms.
>
> (*Poems*, II, 210)

Gratuitous references to Jews of this sort mark Donna Clara's remarks in each set of question-answer. When the knight asks Donna Clara if her heart looks on him with favor, she swears her love "by our Saviour, / Whom the accursed Jews did murder. . . ." Then the knight asks whether his beloved ever swore falsely, to which she replies:

> "Naught is false, in me, my darling,
>   E'en as in my veins there floweth
> Not a drop of blood that's Moorish,
>   Neither of foul Jewish current."

> "Heed not Moors nor Jews, beloved,"
>   Spake the knight with fond endearments.
>   (*Poems*, II, 211)

Finally, the knight leads her to a grove of myrtles where love's passion overcomes all fears and resistance. They sleep. A burst of music awakens them, and Donna Clara is about to rush back into the hall when she asks her paramour's name. Amidst gentle laughter and many kisses, he replies:

> "I, Señora, your beloved,
>   Am the son of the respected
> Worthy, erudite Grand Rabbi,
>   Israel of Saragossa."

>   (*Poems*, II, 212)

With this gross and pointed irony, the ballad concludes.

Apparently, however, Heine did not intend to end the story of Donna Clara at this point. Lazarus quotes from Heine's correspondence, where the poet reveals his intention to write a trilogy in which the son conceived in this illicit moment grows up hating Jews and then, becoming a Dominican monk, cruelly persecutes them.[9] Heine never completed the plan, but Lazarus announces, "I have endeavored to carry out in the two following original Ballads the Poet's first conception" (*Poems*, II, p. 213). The group was entitled "Donna Clara and Two Imitations."

To judge how closely Lazarus was able to imitate Heine's style in English translation, we might read a few stanzas from the two ballads which form Lazarus's sequel to Heine's "Donna Clara." The plot of the first ballad, "Don Pedrillo," has Donna Clara now living like a nun, frequently "Bringing masses for the needy." To the horror of all, especially her rabidly Jew-hating son, Don Pedrillo, little Pedro, she is occasionally visited by a rabbi. One day, while the boy is teaching anti-Semitic curses to his parrot, the rabbi confronts him:

> Very gentle was his aspect,
>   And his voice was mild and friendly,
> "Evil words, my son, thou speakest,
>   Teaching to the fowls of heaven."

The boy, "no whit abashed," snarls:

> "To your beard I will repeat it,
>   That I only bide my manhood,
> To wreak all my lawful hatred,
>   On thyself and on thy people."
>
>   (*Poems*, II, 216)

Now the dramatic irony begins to build. The rabbi warns the boy that his father may have loved "this people," but Pedrillo cries:

> "Loyal knight was he and noble,
>   And my mother oft assured me,
> Ne'er she saw so pure a Christian
>   'Tis from him my zeal deriveth."

> "What if he were such another [asks the rabbi]
>   As myself who stand before thee?"
> "I should curse the hour that bore me,
>   I should die of shame and horror,"
>
>   (*Poems*, II, 217)

replies Pedrillo.

The final stage of the story is told in the second ballad. As "Fra Pedro," the son is now officially able to fulfill his hatred. The ballad is mainly a conversation between him and a lay brother, the latter pleading with "the abbot, great Fra Pedro" to spare the beloved physician, Ben Jehudah, and his lovely daughter. Three years before, "bribed menials" from the Holy Office had "fired their dwelling," burning mother and another daughter alive. But, declares Pedro,

> 'Tis enough; my vow is sacred
>   These shall perish with their brethren.

> Hark ye! In my veins' pure current
> Were a single drop found Jewish,
>
> I would shrink not from outpouring
> All my life blood, but to purge it.
> Shall I gentler prove to others?
> Mercy would be sacrilegious.

(Poems, II, 222)

Following this climax of irony, Lazarus closes her imitation of Heine with the image of the singing of the Angelus "summoning the monks to vespers." The contrast between the inhumanity of Fra Pedro and the saintliness of Christian prayer needs no elaboration.

Lazarus's success in emulating the technique and tone of Heine in the "Two Imitations" was testified to in her own day by the reviewer in the *Jewish Chronicle*,[10] while another contemporary reviewer, in the *Critic*, found "the music of these verses . . . as fascinating and realistic as the original."[11] A later critic, H. B. Sachs, in *Heine in America* (1917), wrote, "How well she succeeded in imitating and reproducing Heine's manner, tone and sentiment [is] obvious."[12] Arthur Zeiger demurs. He finds Lazarus's imitations "all surface—no depth," and without Heine's "diabolism." She merely moralizes that "unplanted sin may reap a harvest of suffering."[13] But Zeiger misreads Lazarus's intention. She offers no moral, only the bitter irony of anti-Semitism, because she is not in a preaching mood in these ballads, only an ironic one. The Jews are not divinely punished because of the sin of Donna Clara and the Rabbi's son. Their fate results from the virulence of a brat. We cannot even say that Lazarus sees anti-Semitism in these poems as a fighting cause. It appears merely as a vehicle for an exercise in irony. That it probably entered her subconscious as a crime against her and her people is a conjecture supported only by hindsight on our part.

IV *Evaluating the Translator*

As a translator of Heine, Emma Lazarus received high marks indeed. The *Critic* called "Miss Lazarus' version . . . a copy of an artist's work made by an artist's hand. . . . Nothing of the original strength and freshness is lost."[14] Several reviewers were not content with just general statements of admiration; they delved into technical niceties as well. To support his favorable opinion, the reviewer in the *Century* asserted that Lazarus's "renderings from the original are remarkably close, and enjoy the same freedom from involution or straining after effect." However, he, like one or two modern critics, had reservations about shades of meaning Lazarus had put into several of her lines.[15]

The New York Times noted that Lazarus adeptly gave Heine's rhymed German the weight of cadence and rhythm, and the unrhymed lines the weight of vowel and accents—a more difficult matter and not always successful. This reviewer hoped that a translator who had "such a knack of catching just the rhythms of the artfully simple lays of Heine" would publish more translations of his work.[16] H. B. Sachs found "her rhymes . . . for the most part exact" and "with considerable success" reproduced the "limpidity . . . and subtle suggestiveness of the original." [17] Finally, Albert Mordell felt that her "fidelity to the spirit of the original . . . read[s] not like translations but like magnificent originals." [18]

Probably it is the conventional nineteenth-century diction that has discouraged twentieth-century editors of Heine-in-translation from using more of Lazarus's versions. Nonetheless, her aptitude and joy in translating him are evident and communicated to the reader.

V   Understanding Heine

Emma Lazarus wrote two essays on Heine—the first as the Introduction to the Poems and Ballads, the other, entitled "The Poet Heine," as a contribution to the Century three years later. Both are biographical as well as critical. The theme of Heine's Jewishness surprisingly becomes the central issue of Lazarus's portrayal of the poet's life. In the Introduction, Lazarus makes obeisance to the fact that Heine was born Jewish and converted only superficially to Lutheranism. She had to be pushed by a reviewer in a general popular journal to recognize the centrality of this fact in Heine's life and work. She did better in the later essay.

We should note that, for some reason, Lazarus avoided translating any of Heine's "Hebrew Melodies." Not one appears among the translations of 1866 in Lazarus's Poems and Translations, or among the ones published in periodicals in ensuing years, or among the Poems and Ballads in 1881. That Heine had emulated another of Lazarus's favorites, Lord Byron, seems not to have had any effect upon her choosing not to translate them. That she herself had begun to translate Hebrew melodies of medieval Jewish poets during this period seems again to have left her unaffected. That Lazarus made any reference at all under these circumstances to Heine's Jewish birth led Rosenfeld to believe that the Introduction was written after the pogroms in Russia became worldwide news.[19]

So we ought not to be surprised that Lazarus deemphasized the Jewish aspect of Heine's life. She treats his birth as a Jew as an objective accident of fate, his championing of Jewish causes as merely a coincidence in his championing of avid liberties for all.[20] She does, however, mention Heine's "Rabbi of Bacharach" as illustrating the persecution of his people during the Middle Ages.[21] (She will adopt the theme of medieval persecution in *The Dance to Death* [1882].) Essentially, though, as her sister Josephine remarked in her memoir, "She is as yet unaware or only vaguely conscious of the real bond between them: the sympathy in the blood, the deep, tragic Judaic passion of eighteen hundred years." [22]

And Lazarus was soundly criticized for this obtuseness, and from a surprising source—not the New York Jewish periodicals that reviewed the book, but the national periodical, *Century*. Its reviewer complained that Lazarus's biographical account lacked "two features": "consideration of Heine from the standpoint of an Israelite" and "how do orthodox Jews regard the scoffing poet." Elaborating, the reviewer says, "Now that the *Judenhetze* is aroused once more in Russia, . . . [a] co-religionist . . . one so well-fitted by birth, education, and a poetical nature as Miss Lazarus should have considered these matters." From a critical point of view, "the main objective would be the consideration of Heine as a Hebrew poet, who used German as his native and French as his adopted, tongue." [23]

Stung by the rebuke, fired by her own reactions to the *Judenhetze* of the next three years, and in the throes of her new inspiration as a poet of Jewish themes, Lazarus corrected her perspective of the life of Heine in "The Poet Heine." [24] What the reviewer taught Lazarus was that ethnic origins of a poet might have an important bearing on his art; that a consideration of ethnicity in art is in no way a contradiction of the quality or the universality of his work; that a contribution to art, culture, and humanism may still, even in the nineteenth century, be made by a poet of a minority group expressing the experience, the consciousness of that group. This was a lesson in democracy that Emma Lazarus had to learn, and learn it she did.

Carefully avoiding any reference to her own personal and artistic development, though she must have realized it paralleled Heine's, in "The Poet Heine" she builds the essay around the proposition that "[Heine] was a Jew with the mind and eyes of a Greek" (210). She reports, "He confesses that in his youth he had never done justice to this great master [Moses on Sinai] nor to the Hebrew people," and quotes, " 'But my predilection for the Hellenic world has diminished since then. I see now that the Greeks were only beautiful youths, whilst the Jews were always men . . . even today, in spite of eighteen centuries of persecution and misery' " (211). This feeling she understood fully. For example, she, like Heine, on the way back to a communion with her ancestral people, had met and translated several poems by Yehuda HaLevi, a rabbi in medieval Spain, on the themes of exile and the revival of Zion, and she, too, was deeply affected by the magic HaLevi exerted over the intervening centuries.

Her attitude as Jewess and Jewish poet, in sum, came to coincide with Heine's. "His sympathy with [Jews]," she summarizes, "was a sympathy of race, not of creed" (216). Heine consigned a greater legacy to a fellow poet than snappy versifying, sentimental poetry, and decadent Romanticism. He contributed to her growing identification with her people, the source for her best and most lasting poetry.

CHAPTER 10

Loomings of a Jewish Consciousness

IN his Preface to *Letters to Emma Lazarus*, Professor Ralph L. Rusk remarks that the poet "[had] kept to current literary models," but "then, in 1882, came a sudden change. . . . She was ready to listen to the suggestion from friends, like [E. C.] Stedman, that she leave the old conventional subjects and try to write of her own people." [1] Stedman himself reported his advice in a letter read at a memorial meeting for Emma Lazarus in 1905. He refers to their frequent meetings in the period 1879 to 1881 and to her complaint that she " 'had accomplished nothing to stir: nothing to awaken. . . . ' " Thereupon he had inquired why she had been indifferent to Jewish inspiration, and she replied that "Hebrew ideals did not appeal to her." The imminent persecutions of Jews in Europe, writes Stedman, touched her off. [2]

The awakening of her Jewish consciousness, however, was really not quite so sudden. It was more a matter of a latent seed developing slowly and sporadically, and suddenly sprouting forth. The stages, in fact, may be traced in poems written over a period of fifteen years.

I *Early Biblical Strains*

The Hebrew Bible, which she was taught as a child in a Jewish household, was the earliest source of what little poetry she wrote that was in any way inspired by her heritage. In her first book of poems appears "Remember" (composed January 20, 1866). It is based on Ecclesiastes 12:1—"Remember then thy Creator in the days of thy youth. Before the evil days come. . . ." In the context of these early conventionally sentimental pieces, it is clear that Lazarus merely found biblical support for a favorite theme—the transiency of time:

> Remember Him, the only One
> Now, e'er the years flow by;

> Now, while the smile is on thy lips,
>   The light within thine eye.

(*Poems and Translations*, p. 54)

Though conventionally "universal," the feeling was deemed true, well-expressed, and "Jewish." Years later, of all the poems published by Lazarus, "Remember" was one of three selected to represent her in the Memorial Issue of the *American Hebrew*. And Rabbi Gustav Gottheil of the Temple Emanuel in New York reprinted it in his *Hymns and Anthems* for his synagogue service.[3]

In July 1867, we might recall, Lazarus penned "In the Jewish Synagogue at Newport," her companion piece to Longfellow's poem. Like Longfellow, she believed that the Hebrews had run their course and that the synagogue was merely a sacred reminder of the glory that was Jerusalem (*Admetus*, 160–62). Though she does show that she had been exposed to postbiblical Jewish history, there is nothing insightful, inspirational, or personal as yet.

Another early poem that has some Biblical inspiration but strikes a more contemporaneous note is "The Valley of Baca." When she was gathering poems for *Songs of a Semite* (1882),[4] Lazarus wrote to Philip Cowen, editor of the *American Hebrew*, that this poem was composed "ten years ago," that is, in 1872, and claimed it was "written off at a sitting . . . & not a line . . . has been altered or 'elaborated' since it was first written."[5] The poem is subtitled Psalm LXXXIV," whose verse 7 reads: "Passing through the valley of Baca they make it a place for springs; yea the early rain clotheth it with blessings."

One translation of the word "Baca" is *tears*, from the Hebrew word for weeping. Lazarus envisions "a brackish lake . . . with bitter pools" through which she sees

> a youth pass down that vale of tears;
> His head was circled with a crown of thorns. . . .

(*Poems*, II, 9)

He persists through the mists and vapors and emerges triumphant. Having undergone so powerful a test, having survived "the valley of the shadow and of death" (equating this valley with one in Psalm 23), "no grief, no fears / Assail him further."

Obviously, the astonishing Christological allusion needs comment. If indeed the poem had been written in 1872, then the reference betokens her universalist thinking of the time. Jesus, with his crown of thorns, is not a sectarian god, but a universal figure of suffering and triumph. However, she later included the poem in a collection that assailed Christianity as a faith that failed its humanist preachments. The poem, then, already betokens a new, developing symbolism. Jesus was ironically to become the symbol of the contemporary Jew suffering at the hands of Jesus' followers, yet rising, like the figure in "The Valley of Baca," above the tribulations visited upon him. In the irony is Lazarus's sense of triumph. She remembered this poem, resurrected it, and included it later in a group of poems that expresses both a new sorrow and a new militancy.[6]

II   *The Call of the "Shofar"*

Lazarus displays a deeper sense of Jewishness in the elegy that she wrote for her uncle, Jacques Judah Lyons, who served her family's synagogue, Shearith Israel, as a cantor for thirty-eight years.[7] "In Memoriam: Rev. J. J. Lyons" was printed in *Lippincott's* in April 1877 and in the *Jewish Messenger* in October of the same year. Five years later, the *American Hebrew* reprinted it, and Lazarus collected it into *Songs of a Semite*. One critic of her day called the poem "the fullest, sweetest, and highest note struck by this young lady." [8] Such a statement alone commends it to our study. Moreover, the poem marks a turning point in the Jewish phase of Lazarus's career. Now she displays a more mature reworking of Jewish source material which betokens a knowledge and a consciousness heretofore not evident.

The poem is dated "Rosh Hashana, 5638"—that is, the autumn of 1877, when Reverend Lyons died. Rosh Hashana is the Jewish observance of New Year, and is characterized by solemnity, prayer, and spiritual introspection. The most striking ritualistic feature of the order of worship is the sounding of the *shofar*, the cornet made from a ram's horn, as a call to repentance—a ritual which has attracted mystical interpretation throughout the centuries.

As the basis of her elegy, Lazarus uses the season of the year in which the holiday is celebrated, the sounding of the *shofar*, and not-inaccurate imaginings of the Temple service in Jerusalem of old. The first stanza envisions:

> The golden harvest-tide is here, the corn
> Bows its proud tops beneath the reaper's hand.
> Ripe orchards' plenteous yields enrich the land,
> Bring first fruits and offer them this morn. . . .

> Sacrifice your best, first fruits to-day.
> With fainting hearts and hands forspent with toil
> Offer the mellow harvest's splendid spoil
> To Him who gives and Him who takes away.
>
> *(Poems*, II, 7)

Only by the allusion to the Jewish burial service in the last line do we perceive the sad, gentle irony that Uncle Lyons is this year's best, first fruit, as it were, the splendid spoil, to be sacrificed to God.[9]

With this solemnized introduction, Lazarus now turns to the most awesome moments of the Rosh Hashana service—the blowing of the ram's horn and the prayer that recounts God's governance of each man's destiny. The prayer book intones, "On Rosh Hashana, it is inscribed . . . who shall live and who shall die; who shall finish his allotted time, and who not; . . . who to remain tranquil, and who be disturbed; who shall reap enjoyment, and who be painfully afflicted. . . ." In these accents, Lazarus chants:

> Sing, holy, holy, holy is the Lord
> Who killeth and who quickeneth again,
> Who woundeth, and who healeth mortal pain,
> Whose hand afflicts us, and who sends us peace. . .
> With the spent year, may the year's sorrows cease.
>
> *(Poems*, II, 7-8)

To this point the elegy strikes a pure, solemn, appropriate note. Now, however, old habits of elegizing come forth, with inferior inversions, poetic archaisms, and conventions of pastoralism.

> Ripe of years was he,
> The priest, the good old man who wrought so well
> Upon his chosen glebe. . .
> What shall be said when such as he do pass?. . .
> But mourn him not, whose blameless life complete
> Rounded its perfect orb. . . .
>
> *(Poems*, II, 8)

Lazarus does not yet know whether she wants to follow in the footsteps of Thomas Gray or Cantor Lyons.

The advance over previous Jewish poetry is seen in the fresh and appropriate use she makes of Hebraic material. She displays much broader knowledge of Judaism and its practice. She is on sure ground when involved with this material—the versifying is apt, interesting, and straightforward, anticipating the later stages of this development, when no artificial influences will intrude anymore.

III *Voices over the Centuries*

It was Rabbi Gustav Gottheil of the Reform Temple Emanuel in New York who acquainted Emma Lazarus with the poetry of medieval Jewish poets of Spain and Portugal. He had asked the most famous Jewish poet of his day in America to translate, from nineteenth-century German translations by Michael Sachs and Abraham Geiger, hymns written by Yehuda HaLevi (1086–1142), Solomon Ibn Gabirol (1021–1070), and Moses Ben Eza (1070–1139).[10] Doubtful at first, she wrote Gottheil on February 6, 1877, "The more I see of these religious poems, the more I feel that the fervor and enthusiasm requisite to their production are altogether lacking in me." But she did inquire whether Gottheil wanted a translation close to the German or "the sacrifice of some of the sense" to permit easier singing.[11] The latter became policy, and later, after her death, her verses were put to music together with the other hymns in Gottheil's hymnal. Perhaps what attracted her to the project after all was curiosity, curiosity fed by the fact that these poets flourished in her father's family's ancestral homeland so long ago.

She translated three poems in 1877: HaLevi's "Admonition," Ibn Gabirol's "Meditation on Death," and Ben Ezra's "In the Night." Although all were hymns composed for specific synagogue services on holy days, they all in some measure expressed Lazarus's old favorite themes of the transiency of Time and the coming of Death. "Admonition," in fact, reprises the theme of her own "Remember," written a decade earlier than this translation:

> Long in the lap of childhood didst thou sleep
> Think how thy youth like chaff did disappear,
> Shall life's sweet Spring forever last?

HaLevi, however, completes his thought with a religious admonition absent from Lazarus's early poetry:

> Drawn near to God, His holy angels know,
> For whom His bounteous streams of mercy flow.[12]

"Meditation on Death," by Gabirol, also sounds much like Lazarus's own poems on this subject. Indeed, imagery and occasional aphorisms recall hers:

> Forget thine anguish
>   Vexed heart, again.
> Why shoulds't thou languish,
>   With earthly pain? . . .
> The husk shall slumber,
>   Bedded with clay
> Silent and sombre
>   Oblivion's prey!
>
> Of all thou didst have,
> Follows naught to the grave.
>   Thou fliest thy nest,
> Swift as a bird to thy place of rest. . . .
>
> (*Poems*, II, 180)

Gabirol, a rabbi like HaLevi, now inserts his moral admonition:

> Seek God, oh my soul! . . .
> Pray to Him when all's still,
>   Performing his will. . .
> And so shall the angel of peace by thy warden,
> And guide thee at last to the heavenly garden.
>
> (*Poems*, II, 181–2)

Ben Ezra's "In the Night" begins:

> Unto the house of prayer my spirit yearns,
> Unto the sources of her being turns,
> To where the sacred light of heaven burns,
> She struggles thitherward by day and night
>
> (*Poems*, II, 201)

The spirit (personified throughout the poem) submits to the admission of sin, anguish of guilt, and the glory of God—none of which Emma Lazarus was wont to emulate. But Ben Ezra does express sentiments that Lazarus often poetized. For example—

> For tears my burden seem to lighten best,
> Could I but weep my heart's blood, I might rest.
> My spirit bows with mighty grief oppressed,
> I utter forth my prayer within the night.
>
> Youth's charm has like a fleeting shadow gone,
> With eagle wings the hours of life have flown.

> Alas! the time when pleasure I have known
> I may not now recall by day or night. . . .
>
> (*Poems*, II, 203)

Here are kindred poets, indeed, regardless of their Jewish ortho-
doxy.

After publishing about two dozen brief translations of medieval
Jewish poets in the next four years, Lazarus sent to Gottheil on June
29, 1881, "a large and beautiful collection [of translations] . . . not
made use of in print." [13] In his reply, the Rabbi returned the new
translations together with the trio from 1877 for her to check through
for eventual selection. Referring to the earliest translations, Lazarus
wrote back: "I do not remember a single line nor a single circumstance connected with them and if it were not that I saw my own
handwriting, I could not believe they were my work." [14] Astonishing!

How to explain this sentence? Perhaps, in the course of translating
many more poems, she simply forgot these. Perhaps, were she to
have been shown early Heine translations, she might have said the
same. During this period of time she was busy as well on such diverse
projects as "Comoedia," "Grotesque," "Phaon," translations from
Goethe, nature lyrics for *Lippincott's*, and the story "The Eleventh
Hour."

Nevertheless the road back to Jewish consciousness was opened by
the translations of 1877, and two years later she picked up where she
didn't even remember she had left off.

IV   *What Is Man?*

For seven consecutive Fridays in January and February 1879, the
Jewish Messenger printed Emma Lazarus's translations (via the German of Geiger) of additional poems by HaLevi and Ibn Gabirol. Two
themes dominate this spurt of interest in these poets: the concept of
Man, and the return to Zion.

On January 31, 1879, the *Messenger* printed Lazarus's version of
Gabirol's hymn "Lord, what is Man," inspired by Psalm 144 (verse
3ff.), as a confessional for Yom Kippur, the Jewish Day of Atonement.
All seven stanzas begin "Almighty! what is man?" and each recounts,
respectively, his mortality, weakness, hypocrisy, lust, guilt, and
haughtiness. Finally, Gabirol concludes:

> Then spare him! let him love and mercy win,
> According to thy grace and not according to his sin!
>
> (*Poems*, II, 184)

That Lazarus saw herself still the impartial if passionate product of universal culture is attested to by the curious circumstance that, at precisely the same time that she published this poem by a medieval Jewish poet, in a manuscript poem dated February, 1879, she took another view of man—one she found in a Mohawk fable! The fable tells of a parliament of animals debating which breed shall devise the new creature. Each envisions him as an image of himself, each insisting on including his own best feature until "a scene of wild confusion / Marked the meeting's dissolution." All fall asleep but one—the coyote. He creates man—

> Blest with wit to overreach
> Power & craft of all and each
> Thus according to his plan,
> The coyote fashioned man.

The juxtaposition of Jewish and heathen materials seems to indicate that Lazarus responded to Gabirol's confessional because it contained characteristics so like her own poetry—sentiment, honesty, abasement, and hope; but the sly humor of the Mohawk legend appealed to her sense of irony as well. In any case, five years later, in a poem dated May 1884,[15] she turned back to Jewish materials for a third try at this subject: "The Birth of Man: A Legend of the Talmud."

This legend expresses the opposing ways of evaluating man and mediates between them. On one side, the angel Mercy begs God to "fulfill . . . thine exalted thought." On the other side, the angel Peace weeps that man will bring "confusion, trouble, discord, war." Truth joins Peace and warns, "Father of Truth / . . . Thou brings't / Upon the earth the fallen of all lies!" But God decrees, to the horror of Heaven, that Truth shall accompany man on earth as his companion:

> From heaven to earth, from earth once more to
>   heaven,
> Shall Truth, with constant interchange, alight
> And soar again, an everlasting link
> Between the world and sky.
>   And man was born.
>
> (*Poems*, II, 24–25)

Having arrived at this *modus vivendi*, Lazarus drops the theme, seemingly satisfied with the Talmud's realistic but idealistic view.

V   *Return to Zion*

We may conjecture with what pleasurable wonder Emma Lazarus discovered that Yehuda HaLevi, an eleventh-century rabbi, was human enough to write love poetry. She translated a lovely epithalamion, "A Letter to His Friend Isaac" (*Jewish Messenger*, February 7, 1879) which utilizes, as Lazarus was wont to do, the fable of the seasons to imagize a love relationship:

> But yesterday the earth drank like a child
>   With eager thirst the autumn rain.
> Or like a wistful bride who waits the hour
>   Of love's mysterious bliss and pain.
> And now the Spring is here with yearning eyes.
>
> (*Poems*, II, 190)

HaLevi's "Love Song" has a lass candidly declare:

> "See'st thou o'er my shoulders falling,
>   Snake-like ringlets waving free?
> Have no fear, for they are twisted
>   To allure thee unto me."
>
> (*Poems*, II, 192)

The subtle humorous irony of "Have no fear" undoubtedly appealed to a fellow worker in poetic irony, especially on the theme of love.

In all probability, Lazarus knew of Heinrich Graetz's evaluation of HaLevi's poetry in his monumental *Geschichte der Juden* [*The History of the Jews*] (1853–75). Writes Graetz, "He had a more correct conception of poetry, which he valued as something holy and God-given, than had his Arab and Jewish contemporaries. . . . As long as he was young, he dissipated the gold of his rich poetry on light, flimsy themes. . . . He sang of wine and pleasure. . . ." But, Graetz continues, "the importance of Jehuda HaLevi as a poet lies in those poems that breathe a national–religious spirit. In these his ideas burst from the depths of his heart, his whole being rises upwards in ecstasy, and when he sings of Zion and its past and future glory, when he veils his head in mourning over its present slavery, we find the true spirit of his poetry." [16]

Here was an object lesson for Lazarus to follow, exactly the path from exquisite love poetry to poetry that mattered. Though not quite the kind of poetry of the Real that Emerson had prescribed for her years before, yet it was the kind of inspiration advocated for her by her new preceptor, E. C. Stedman.

For HaLevi, Zion, the city of Jerusalem, is that inspiration, and his poetry expresses the Jewish people's love for the city they lost a thousand years before he lived but never forgot. Lazarus translated HaLevi's "Longing for Jerusalem" in a way that displays her understanding of his passionate love:

LONGING FOR JERUSALEM

Oh, City of the world, with sacred splendor blest,
My spirit yearns to thee from out the far-off West,
A stream of love wells forth when I recall thy day,
Now is the temple waste, thy glory passed away.
Had I an eagle's wings, straight would I fly to thee,
Moisten thy holy dust with wet cheeks streaming free.
Oh! how I long for thee! Albeit thy King has gone,
Albeit where balm once flowed, the serpent dwells alone.
Could I but kiss thy dust, so would I fain expire,
As sweet as honey then, my passion, my desire!

(Poems, II, 193–94)

Perhaps the most important consequence of these songs of Zion was the introduction into Lazarus's mind that a homeland in Palestine was the final, best solution for the exiled Jewish people. Here were poets who saw the Return as not only possible, but obligatory. It was not a mere messianic dream, but an ever-contemporaneous reality, and HaLevi gave his talent and his life to prove it. The idea became a major theme in the fiery essays Lazarus was soon to write.

VI   *The Specter of Persecution*

The theme of anti-Semitic persecution now rises as a major motif in her work. Preparing the *Poems and Ballads* of Heine, Lazarus read but did not include his poem of medieval persecution, "The Rabbi of Bacharach," but she wrote the "Two Imitations" dealing with persecution of Jews. Now came two of her own poems on this subject— "Raschi in Prague" (March 25, 1880) and its sequel, "Death of Raschi" (April 8).[17]

Rashi (1040–1105; commonly spelled without the "c") is the greatest of biblical exegetes and Talmudic clarifiers, bar none, to this very day. He was a grammarian, legalist, and textual critic. Rashi lived all his adult life in France. He got to Prague only in legend, by some fluke of identification perhaps with the wandering messianic prophet, Elijah. That legends should arise around this scholarly figure was strange; that Lazarus found them is even more strange.[18] What attracted her was the sad stories of persecution they told and how Rashi emerges as the hero-martyr.

"Raschi in Prague" is told in blank verse, and, as we found in her earlier blank verse, Lazarus displays an ease of narration, a liquidity of line, and a freedom from artificiality of syntax contorted by rules of rhyme. Characterization, however, does not exist. All characters are unidimensional, as in the case of Rashi himself:

> From his clear eye youth flamed magnificent;
> Force, masked by grace, moved in his balanced frame;
> An intellectual, virile beauty reigned
> Dominant on domed brow, on fine, firm lips,
> An eagle profile cut in gilded bronze. . . .
> Above all beauty of the body and brain
> Shone beauty of a soul benign with love.
>
> (*Poems*, II, 26)

After a triumphant tour of all the major centers of Jewish exile, including a mythical meeting with the great Moses Maimonides (who in reality was born thirty years after Rashi died), Rashi comes to Prague. He is greeted by the adoration of thousands, including Rabbi Jochanan, in whose home he abides.

Now, Rabbi Jochanan has a daughter, typically named Rebekah. Only a charming epic simile comparing her to the biblical Rebekah can serve Lazarus's idealization of her:

> Young, beautiful as her namesake when she brought
> Her firm, frail pitcher balanced on her neck
> Unto the well, and gave the strangers drink,
> And gave his camels drink. The servant set
> The sparkling jar's refreshment from his lips
> And saw the virgin's face, bright as the moon
> Beam from the curled luxuriance of black locks,
> And cast-back linen veil's soft-folded cloud. . . .
>
> (*Poems*, II, 32)

But the advisers to the Duke cannot stomach the Jews' joy, and persuade him to permit a pogrom. Lazarus's description of the pogrom mixes outrage with powerful narration (with aid from *The Merchant of Venice*, I, iii, 113, 118), qualities that were to feature her essays and poems dealing with contemporary pogroms in Europe:

> With one huge crash
> The strong doors split asunder, pouring in
> A stream of soldiers, ruffians, armed with pikes,
> Lances and clubs—the unchained beast, the mob. . . .
> Then, while some stuffed their pokes with baubles snatched
> From board and shelf, or with malignant sword
> Slashed the rich Orient rugs, the pictured woof
> That clothed the wall; others had seized and bound,
> And gagged from speech, the helpless, aged man;
> Still others outraged, with coarse, violent hands,
> The marble-pale, rigid as stone, strange youth [Rashi] . . .
> He struggled not while his free limbs were tied,
> His beard plucked, torn and spat upon his robe. . . .
>
> (*Poems*, II, 33–34)

The Rabbi and Rashi, "Befouled with mud, with raiment torn, wild hair/ And ragged beard" (*Poems*, II, 35), are dragged forth to be thrust contemptuously before the Duke and Bishop.

It turns out that the Bishop recognizes Rashi as the youth who doctored him in Palestine when he had fallen ill on a pilgrimage. The Bishop intervenes; Rashi joins in the plea to the Duke, speaking in the accents of Shylock:

> Grace for my tribe! They are what ye have made.
> If any be among them fawning, false
> Insatiable, revengeful, ignorant, mean—
> And there are many such—ask your own hearts
> What virtues ye would yield for planted hate,
> Ribald contempt, forced, menial servitude,
> Slow centuries of vengeance for a crime
> Ye never did commit?
>
> (*Poems*, II, 38)

Then turning to Rabbi Jochanan, Rashi cries:

> Was that benignant, venerable face
> Fit target for their foul throat's voided rheum?
> That wrinkled flesh made to be pulled and pricked.
> Wounded by flinty pebbles and keen steel?
> Behold the prostrate, patriarchal form,
> Bruised silent. chained. Duke, such is Israel!
>
> (*Poems*, II, 39)

The Duke frees them and stops the pogrom.

Albert Mordell sees the poem as contrasting the morality and spirituality of the Jew with the coarseness and materialism of the gentile,[19] something about to be reflected in the Heine imitations. Arthur Zeiger thinks "Raschi in Prague" "easily the best and most original poem that Emma Lazarus wrote from the beginning of her career to 1880." [22] Finally, in theme and execution, Lazarus had caught fire.

The sequel, "The Death of Raschi" is a severe falling off. Rashi and Rebekah are now married. During the Passover Seder, when the ritual requires the opening of the door to symbolize faith in God's control of Israel's enemies, Rashi is stabbed and dies. However, Rebekah revives him by means of herbs and love. To fool the murderers, an empty coffin is buried, and Rashi lives to do his holy work (*Poems*, II, 40–44). The poem is a dramatic monologue, but Zeiger's comment that it is "after the fashion of Browning" is too kind.[21] The poem lacks characterization of the monologuist and of his listener; it lacks richness of atmosphere, the suggestive gesture, the telling detail, the unwittingly revealing expression.

We go back to "Raschi in Prague" for the turning point of Emma Lazarus's slow return to her ethnic heritage. The anger, the indignation, the sense of Christian treachery to their own teaching, as well as to their Jewish origin, mark the dissolution of the barrier between the poet's dedication to alien culture and the destiny of her people.

CHAPTER 11

Power in Prose

BETWEEN 1882 and 1884, Emma Lazarus wrote twenty-two essays and two brief editorials on Jewish matters. Some are reasoned expositions of the problems and possibilities in relocating European Jewry to Palestine; others are personal essays on aspects of Jewish life, like the Sabbath; a few are indignant reactions to instances of anti-Semitism in America, like the refusal of a hotel room to a Jew in Boston; several others, which will concern us most, are polemical in their discussion of Jewish topics.

Interestingly, nearly all her fiery verse on these subjects followed the publication of two of these argumentative essays, "Was the Earl of Beaconsfield a Representative Jew?" and "Russian Christianity versus Modern Judaism" in April and May 1882, respectively. It would seem that she had to prime her mind and heart in prose before she could blaze forth in poetry the turbulence in her as current Jewish history unfolded. These two essays are actually animadversions on essays by others, and for a moment the bellicose spirit of Milton and the seventeenth century gleams.

I The Example of Disraeli

Among those who, in latter years, served as examples to Emma Lazarus as latent Jews who contributed to art and mankind was Benjamin Disraeli, the former Prime Minister of England, the Earl of Beaconsfield, the son of Jewish parents converted to Christianity, himself baptized at the age of twelve. A year or so after his death in 1881, an article about him by James Bryce, a member of Parliament, appeared in the *Century* for March 1882.[1] While discussing Disraeli's background, Bryce mentions his Jewish origins as merely a point of interest, not as a "reproach upon him." This mild snobbishness no doubt pricked Emma Lazarus. She was also attracted by another point Bryce made, that Jews "are prone to mockery" because of centuries of scorn which "in Heinrich Heine mingled itself with a poet's tenderness." Knowing a thing or two about Heine, Lazarus interested herself mightily in Bryce's hypotheses.

Bryce found in Disraeli "three . . . characteristics of his race in full measure—detachment, intensity, scorn." "He felt himself no Englishman," asserts Bryce, and he watched English life and politics like a naturalist observing the habits of bees or ants. "A greater source of strength lay in his Hebrew intensity. It would have pleased him, so full of pride in the pure blood of his race, to attribute to that purity the singular power of concentration which the Jews undoubtedly possess." An example, "in proportion to their numbers, of an unusually large number of able and successful men," Disraeli reached his pinnacle "by patient and unaided efforts" and, though "his aims were mainly selfish," brought England to its supreme position in the world.

Bryce's article, however, was only the catalyst solidifying Lazarus's thinking about another study of Disraeli, George Brandes's *Lord Beaconsfield* (1880). Brandes concluded that, because Disraeli lacked idealism but had the persistence, industry, pragmatism, wit, and ambition "of his race," he was a "typical representative." [2]

What did these Darwinian views of the Jewish species mean to Emma Lazarus? First, they reminded her that Jews had survived into the nineteenth century *as* a species, not merely as vestiges of a former people; second, they had developed over millenia of persecution characteristics not only for survival but for power and contribution. It was to clarify the latter point that she wrote "Was the Earl of Beaconsfield a Representative Jew?" [3]

Annoyed by intimations that Disraeli was, as she said, a "Shylock," Lazarus tried to balance him with the qualities of a "Spinoza" as well. Around this comparison/contrast she organizes her essay. No one man, Lazarus points out, can contain *all* characteristics of these two figures—Spinoza's "combination of mysticism and cool-headed shrewdness, of powerful imagination and mathematical precision . . . together with indomitable energy, unhesitating self-confidence and indefatigible perserverance" (939); and Shylock's "poetic, oriental imagination dealing in tropes and symbols, the energy, or rather now the obstinancy, of will, the intellectual superiority, the peculiarly Jewish strength of national and domestic sentiments . . . the astuteness, the sarcasm, the pathos, the egotism, and the cunning of the Hebrew usurer" (939–40). Disraeli, however, had enough of each type to be considered a representative Jew (942).

The argument is weak. It is not very logical or historical to discuss the nature of the Jewish people by referring to one actual figure and to one fictional character—the latter created, indeed, by a non-Jew! In itself, the character of Shylock has been "typified" by so medieval an attitude as to make it nearly a caricature. Nothing can be argued from that. Morever, as Cyrus L. Sulzberger pointed out in a brief rejoinder to Lazarus's animadversion on the Brandes-Bryce view, "The most absurd proposition can be thoroughly proved" on the basis of her Spinoza-Shylock typification, because it describes all human beings on earth.[4]

But Lazarus nearly managed it, first of all because she prepared herself. Here is no maudlin dip into poetic imagination. She marshals history and personalities, events and quotations in quite an un-Romantic way. To equate Spinoza and Shylock shows a cleverness of argumentation that uses research in imaginative contexts. Her argument strikes one as if it ought to be right. Furthermore, she developed a persuasive style based on the periodic sentence that harks back to classical oratorical tradition, rather than to the literary tradition of English prose. For example:

Where shall we look for the great modern Jews? At the head of the revolutions, the politics, the finance, the journalism of Europe, among actors, musical *virtuosi* and composers, wherever they can find a field for their practical ability, their long starved appetite for power, their love of liberty, and their manifold talents (941–42).

This is powerful rhetoric that has the functional structure of the Baconian sentence, without its pretty turns and balances. Lazarus here writes a prose of rising action of oral argumentation that was found admirable in the Roman Senate and in Disraeli's own House of Commons.

But Sulzberger's criticism had a deeper effect in a different direction than merely straightening Lazarus out on the Shylock-Spinoza silliness. All men have characteristics of Spinoza and Shylock, he wrote, but "the representative man of the Jewish race is a representative Jew, when his life and his works are marked by Jewish thought, by sympathy with Israel's past and Israel's future, by interest in Israel's trials and Israel's successes."[5] Thus he defined for Lazarus— and, by the way, for future Jewish writers in America—what makes a story or a poem peculiarly "Jewish." Not its general humanism nor its sentiment—that's what makes it part of the world's literature—but its identifiable ethnic characteristics. Sulzberger directed Emma Lazarus away from searching for the typicality of the Jew to perceiving his uniqueness.

One passage in "Was the Earl of Beaconsfield a Representative Jew?" indicates that Lazarus would be an apt pupil. She expresses for the first time a pride in her own distinctive Sephardi Jewish ancestry. She quotes "an English writer" on the history of the Sephardim describing their intellectual eminence when Ashkenazim were living "amid the ferocity and unlettered ignorance of Muscovy and Poland." Proudly she declares, "There can be no doubt that a spark of fiery Castilian pride was transmitted, unstifled by intervening ages of oppression, to the spirit of Benjamin Disraeli" (941).

The spark of fiery Castilian pride was about to flame in Emma Lazarus—but, ironically, it was the plight of the Ashkenazim of Muscovy and Poland that ignited it.

II *An Essay of Outrage*

During the last few months of 1881, London and New York newspapers carried eye-witness stories of horrendous pogroms in Germany and especially Russia. Despatches describing the Russian mobs' descent into destruction, barbarism, murder, and wantonness were controlled only by the genteel standards of nineteenth-century journalism. But the accounts were horrific enough. Reaction was not long in becoming vocal. Meetings and demonstrations were held in New York and committees were organized to aid the flow of refugees from Russia that began to reach the U.S. immigration station on Ward's Island in New York harbor. Condemnation was universal.

In April 1882, the *Century Magazine* received an article by a respected Russian woman social scientist, Mme. Z. Ragozin, defending the character of the rampaging mobs. It was a defense based on an unsympathetic description of the Jewish character. Because of its "open columns" policy, the *Century* printed it.[6]

The behavior of the Russian peasants, Ragozin says, was admirable in its restraint and commendable for its selectivity:

It was a good natured mob . . . which did not provoke violence by resistance [to the troops]. . . . It destroyed only property and could be dissuaded from destroying Jewish domiciles if the Jew was a doctor or had a good reputation. . . . The worst instincts of a mob were not called into play, in great part owing to the prudence of the Jews themselves, who mostly kept out of sight (906).

Ragozin goes on to accuse the Russian Jewish community of economically enslaving the Russian peasant. Nor is this merely a local condition; it is the standard, organized method of the Jewish canker, as described by the notorious Jewish apostate, Jacob Branfman. It is Branfman's testimony that Ragozin uses to describe these nefarious deeds, allegedly ordered by a central body called "The Kehilla" (913).

Before printing the essay, R. W. Gilder, the editor of the *Century*, showed the essay to Lazarus, who was horrified. He urged her to contribute a refutation, which she did. Her animadversion was printed the next month. From the methods of argumentation that she uses, it is clear that Lazarus had come to believe that anti-Semitism is a disease that cannot be cured by mere logic or rationally correcting the perverted scholarship of the anti-Semite. One must use scorn, ridicule, and sarcasm in addition. In "Russian Christianity versus Modern Judaism," [7] Lazarus uses both the rational and emotional approaches.

In the first place, Lazarus demonstrates, Ragozin is no scholar. How can she believe Branfman's misconceptions about centralization animalizing the Jewish community? Lazarus brings an array of evidence to show that centralization was strongest in Germany, but it in no way interfered with the process of emancipation of German Jews. And yet, Lazarus complains, after a half-century of emancipation the *Judenhetze* began in Europe in the land of Germany! The same anti-Jewish outcry is heard there "as in primitive Russia" (49). Thus, Lazarus implies, the cause of anti-Semitism is in the heart of host, not in the actions of the guests, the Jews. Surprised that a scholar generalizes so fallaciously about the character of the Jewish race, Lazarus replies: "The dualism of the Jews is the dualism of humanity; they are made up of the good and the bad. May not Christendom be divided into those Christians who denounce such outrages as we are considering, and those who commit or apologize for them?" (49). With this touch of scornful *ad hominem* argument, Lazarus turns to other points in Ragozin's essay.

Lazarus's deepest scorn is reserved for Ragozin's defense of the Russian mob. Quoting from the London *Times*, she destroys Ragozin's benign picture of what happened: "Murder, rape, arson, one hundred thousand families reduced to homeless beggary and the destruction of eighty million dollars' worth of property,—such, in fewest words, are the acts for which an excuse is sought" (48). She permits herself to be nearly choked by disbelief in the suggestion that the "simpletons . . . did not know they were committing a blameable act! *Sancta simplicitas!* what precious innocents these Russians must be!" (55–56).

In this essay, Lazarus uses every rhetorical device of scorn and indignation that Cicero taught the Western world to use—sarcasm and ridicule in the correction of the opponent's facts, salvos of facts from one's own arsenal, and the assumption of pained regret that so estimable an opponent would stoop so low as to espouse such a degraded cause. It was an effective reply, and the polemical blood now flowing she injected into the poems she began to write at this time and to more essays that flowed from her pen.

III *Storm over Zion*

From November 1882 to February 1883, Lazarus published in the *American Hebrew* fourteen essays under the general title, "An Epistle to the Hebrews." This title is obviously a parody of St. Paul's epistle in the New Testament. Recent events proved to Lazarus that a new epistle to the Hebrews was necessary, and she undertook to write it. The Prospectus for the series (November 3, 1882) announced her intention "to bring before the Jewish public . . . facts and critical observations . . . [in order] to arouse a more logical and intelligent estimate of the duties of the hour." This she does by essays on Jewish history, culture, and especially the theme of the return to Palestine.

One of the more fascinating aspects of these pieces is the fact that Lazarus excoriates her fellow American Jews for traveling on the path of assimilation, a path that she had just left. This theme represents an agonizing reappraisal of the very sources of her most popular poetry. It resulted in her declaration (December 22, 1882) that "nineteen Christian centuries is not sufficient to protect us in the old world." The fountainhead of modern culture was poisoned in her mind, and even classical culture appeared to be relatively empty, if not suspect.

This shock caused her to become a Zionist a decade before Zionism received its impetus as an organized movement under the dynamism of Theodor Herzl. In an essay of December 8, 1882, she considered the establishment of a homeland for all Jews (except those in America) in Palestine as the final solution. This dream she found expressed in the novel *Daniel Deronda*, by George Eliot, to whom she was therefore to dedicate the verse drama called *The Dance to Death* in her *Songs of a Semite*. She compared this dream to those of Garibaldi and Washington—visionaries, yes, but practical fathers of countries, too. "There is not the slightest necessity for an American Jew, the free citizen of a republic, to rest his hopes upon the foundation of any other nationality" she declared, but the American Jew should contribute financially to such a reality (December 15, 1882). Thus she anticipated American Jewish philanthropy for this purpose by more than half a century.

Not all Jews were ripe in those days for the call to Zionism. The *Jewish Messenger*, a journal which for fifteen years had been publishing Lazarus's poetry, now turned on her. In the editorial for the January 26, 1883, issue, it praised the review of Jewish history in her epistles but deplored her descent from the pristine pedestal of poetry to misguided involvement in political matters. The *Messenger* maintained that this nationalistic notion showed Jews to be "strangers and aliens in Europe and America; patriots only in Palestine."

Lazarus's reply to this attack came in an essay entitled "The Jewish Problem," and was published in the *Century* for February 1883.[8] In one way, the answer contains a surprise. After an impassioned rehearsal of historic crimes against the Jews, Lazarus addresses herself to the charge that she lacks patriotism for America. We might expect, from the fact that she excluded American Jews from the call to emigration to Palestine, that she would hang her patriotism on her sleeve and wave it. However, Lazarus declares that in America every Jew knows that the host society never equates the Jewish community with the best Jews; rather security for the Jew is dependent on the conduct of "the meanest rascal who belongs to the tribe" (608).

She goes on: the American Jew enjoyed "absolute civil and political freedom . . . *until the last few years*" (her italics). Now "everlasting prejudice is cropping out" in the form of boycotts in resorts, schools and universities. "The word 'Jew' is in constant use, even among so-called refined Christians, as a term of opprobrium, and is employed as a verb, to denote the meanest tricks" (608). The disillusionment which marked her view of Christian Europe now seems to be creeping into her view of Christian America. The answer is not assimilation, which was tried in so many European societies and was rejected even by the most enlightened of them, like that of Germany. For her, there is only one answer: "[*The Jews*] *must establish an independent nationality*" (610; her italics).

Such persistence in the face of criticism within her own community shows that she has learned that patriotism does not come in the form of slavish and obsequious panegyrics. It requires also the courage of criticism. That this lady poet who was well known for her antiseptic and innocuous, if adept, verses could, in Victorian America, be capable of such public outbursts astonished many people, but not those who knew Emma Lazarus best. The editors of the journals she wrote for knew that a righteous audacity fashioned essays of passion and argumentative eloquence of a high moral and stylistic order.

CHAPTER 12

Climactic Songs

R EADERS who subscribed to the *American Hebrew* and *Jewish Messenger* weeklies in 1882 had already read the original poems and the translations that were collected later in the year into a slim book of eighty pages entitled *Songs of a Semite*.[1] The first half of the book is devoted entirely to *The Dance to Death*, "a tragedy in five acts," serialized earlier in the *Hebrew*. The rest of the book contains six poems on current Jewish events, a monologue of an incident in past Jewish history, "Donna Clara" and the "Two Imitations" from the *Poems and Ballads* of Heine, and translations of HaLevi, Ibn Gabriol, and Moses Ben Ezra, all reprinted. Now in book form, however, they reached a wider and more influential audience, which included critics in general magazines and newspapers.

I *A Drama of Persecution*

The Dance to Death, as Emma Lazarus's note says (*Poems*, II, 172), is a dramatization of Richard Reinhard's prose narrative, *Der Tanz Zum Tode* (1877), of the martyrdom of the Jews of Nordhausen, Germany, May 4–6, 1349. Lazarus's version is so close to Reinhard that Zeiger judges it largely a translation,[2] but the reviewer in *Lippincott's* anticipated this comment: "Even supposing it to be a result of study and imitation rather than of creative force," the display "of sympathy and discernment . . . cannot be lacking in originality."[3]

Lazarus apparently wrote the play in her first immersion into Jewish subjects in 1879–80, for it owes something to "Rabbi of Bacharach" by Heine, whom she was translating at the time. On May 25, 1882. Lazarus suggested to Philip Cowen, editor of the *American Hebrew*, that he find place for it in the magazine "in order to arouse sympathy and to emphasize the cruelty of the injustice done to our unhappy people."[4] He ran it in ten installments, from June 30 to September 1, 1882.

It also owes some inspiration to George Eliot. Emma Lazarus dedicated *The Dance to Death* to the memory of the English novelist for "elevating and ennobling the spirit of Jewish nationality" (*Poems*, II, 69). This is a clear reference to *Daniel Deronda* (1876), of course, but the play has, in fact, nothing to do with the Zionist theme which is featured in that novel. In the light of Lazarus's career as a polemical essayist, we might suppose that more inspiration came from George Eliot's essay "The Modern Hep-Hep," [5] a scathing attack on renascent anti-Semitism in Europe.

The drama opens *in medias res* and in the classic manner of exposition. Two Jewish burghers, minor figures in the action, in natural conversation give us the necessary information about the community of Nordhausen, the coming of Rabbi Cresslin, the importance of the wealthy Susskind von Orb, and the non-Jewish beauty of his purported daughter, Leibhaid. Immediately, Lazarus introduces one of the chief tonal qualities of the play, dramatic irony. "I trace not either parent / in her face . . . ," says Naphtali, one of the burghers, heavily foreshadowing things to come.

Rabbi Cresslin, blind from viewing the systematic destruction of Jewish communities of France and Germany, has come to Nordhausen to warn the complacent Jewish community, but they ignore him. Meanwhile, the town's protector, Duke Frederich, is being persuaded by one Henry Schatzen to permit a total pogrom, an intention which is publicly announced to the Jewish community. Schatzen, however, is really aiming for the death of one Jew, Susskind Von Orb, who years before had destroyed his castle. What he does not know (but the audience finds out in an obvious dose of dramatic irony) is that Susskind saved Schatzen's daughter and secretly has cared for her as if she were his own child. The Duke's son, William, falls in love with her, though he thinks her a Jewess, and to him Susskind entrusts a sealed letter which he thinks will save the Jews. William, however, does not use it because his father imprisons him for loving a Jewess. Meanwhile, Schatzen's enemies, Prior Peppercorn and Nordmann, plot his undoing. By chance, Peppercorn, William's confessor also, gets hold of Von Orb's letter, suppresses it, and kidnaps William to keep him out of the way.

The day of the martyrdom arrives. No amount of pleading saves the Jews. At the behest of their rabbi and Susskind, they dress in all their finery to partake in the dance to death that will liberate them from this hateful world. As the fires of the auto-da-fé consume them, William arrives and convinces Schatzen that he has in effect murdered his own daughter. Schatzen falls unconscious as the curtain falls.

Is Lazarus is writing a panegyric to Jewish martyrdom? Is she saying that anti-Semitism has no religious cause, only personal animus? Is she more interested in intra-Christian perfidy than in Jewish heroism? That the final curtain is given to the scourge of the Jews undergoing a private suffering that temporizes his villainy is a strange bit of dramaturgy. Clearly, Lazarus's dramatic sense, so true in her narrative poems, still fails her in play form. Her obsession with irony affects the plot and the characterization. No character (except for Prior Peppercorn) is natural. Each represents a single quality: Schatzen, villainy; Susskind, nobility; William, romantic (but ineffectual) heroism; Cresslin's daughter and Susskind's "daughter" total purity and filial devotion. No Jew hesitates, once his doom is understood. Only in Peppercorn's character, uniquely, does Lazarus combine a complexity of religious fire, pride, shrewdness, and venality.

And yet, as a drama, *The Dance to Death* is an improvement over *The Spagnoletto* in emotional control and dialogue. In the speeches she gives to the Jewish characters, Lazarus achieves just the right balance of heroism in restraint—no posturing, no flamboyance, just quiet, dignified desperation. Their rabbi instructs them:

> Bring from the Ark, the bell-fringed, silken-bound
> Scrolls of the Law. Gather the silver vessels,
> Dismantle the rich curtains of the doors,
> Bring in the Perpetual Lamp; all these shall burn,
> For Israel's light is darkened, Israel's Law
> Profaned by strangers. . . .
>
> (*Poems*, II, 165)

And, still atoning for once agreeing that dead nations do not rise again, she places in Susskind's mouth these melodramatic (but true) lines:

> We hold
> His Law, His lamp, His covenant, His pledge.
> Wherever in the ages shall arise
> Jew-priest, Jew-poet, Jew-singer, or Jew-saint—
> And everywhere I see them star the gloom—
> In each of these the martyrs are avenged.
>
> (*Poems*, II, 165)

Having found the vehicle of sufficient magnitude to fit the gift for declamation recently discovered in her essays, Lazarus succeeds in leaving her reader with echoes of resounding sentiments. The attempt to give a tone of plausibility to inescapable posturing, Lazarus anticipates twentieth-century verse-drama by T. S. Eliot and Maxwell Anderson. It is only fair to say that she failed with eminent peers.

II *Public Response to* The Dance to Death

Happily, it must be reported, contemporary reactions to *The Dance to Death* ignored nearly all the criticisms made above. *Lippincott's* reviewer nearly said it all when he attributed Lazarus's "dramatic power [of which] she proves herself to be possessed in a high degree" to "the lofty purpose and artistic restraint." He found very impressive the integration of allusions to Jewish worship and English dramatic tradition. What the latter may have been is unclear. Perhaps the reviewer meant the tradition of closet dramatic writing then in vogue, for he found *Dance to Death* a reading, not an acting, play. [6] Perhaps the dramatic tradition he referred to was the broad Senecan tragedy Shakespeare had brought to sublime heights, but which by the late nineteenth century had become bombast beloved of the groundlings Hamlet had despised.

The *New York Sun* reviewer found *Dance to Death* to have "pathos and terror [note the Aristotelian terminology!] . . . strikingly brought out by the careful treatment of incident and graduation of interest. . . . The plot is skillfully evoked." [7] *The Century* agrees: "The plot itself does much to awaken and fascinate the attention." [8] The *Critic*, however, demurs. "The plot is there, fine, not wholly new. . . . The monologue is sometimes too long. . . . The climax is not built up with sufficient power." On the other hand, "the tone is elevated and strong, the diction fresh, and poetic, and vigorous," and Lazarus displays the "dramatic power of putting herself into her characters." [9] Nearly all reviewers found the dialogue impressive and thrilling and the characters impressive. [10] Despite some obscurity in the motivation of some characters, said the *New York Times*, "the ability to handle a matter of this scope is rare, and. . .Miss Lazarus has come near to making a masterpiece of it." [11]

All in all *The Dance to Death* was a triumph, despite its weaknesses. Stedman described it as a "tragedy . . . a work of much power" when he enshrined Lazarus into the pantheon of his *Poets of America*. [12] And Henry Ward Beecher in the *Independent* also called it a "tragedy of remarkable finish and power" (September 28, 1882, p.

13). Finally, as a spokesman of the Jewish reading public, Mayer Sulzberger, paraphrasing Susskind von Orb's lines on the future of the Jewish nation, exulted: "America may proudly glory that hers is the Jew-poet where wide human sympathy has penetrated with equal genius the inner world of Jew and Greek, and Teuton." [13] Thus, Sulzberger, with keen insight into the career of Emma Lazarus, saw *The Dance to Death* as the inevitable culmination of her work.

III   *The Agony of Ages*

The selection of original poems that follows *Dance to Death* in *Songs of a Semite* is a reprise of the themes Lazarus developed in her argumentative essays—indignation against the failure of Christianity and new faith in the Jewish nation that miraculously is no longer dead. [14] Here, the volcanic emotions—deeper than anything she ever felt before—come out more forcefully because of plain poetic compression. This is a poetry quite different from past verse. As *Lippincott's* critic noted, Lazarus used to write with "an air of coldness" owing to "purity and intellect"; now she displays "more impulse." [15]

The lead poem in this group is, appropriately, "The New Year: Rosh Hashana 5643 [September 1882]." But this piece is far different from the serene New Year poem in which she eulogized her uncle a few years earlier. The *shofar*-blast now betokens a crisis in Jewish history:

> Blow Israel, the sacred cornet! Call
>   Back to thy courts whatever faint heart throb
> With thine ancestral blood, thy need craves all.
>   The red, dark year is dead, the year just born
> Leads on from anguish wrought by priest and mob,
>   To what undreamed-of morn?

No doubt Emma Lazarus was also speaking to herself in this call to return to the ancestral bond. The last few years had given her the new perspective to be able to perceive

> In two divided streams the exiles part,
>   One rolling homeward to its ancient source,
> One rushing sunward with fresh will, new heart.
>   By each the truth is spread, the law unfurled.
> Each separate soul contains the nation's force,
>   And both embrace the world.

(Poems, II, 1-2)

The structure of the stanza parallels the theme. One half of a nation
is going home to Zion; the other "rushing sunward," following the sun
westward to the new world. The climax of the stanza brings out the
thought that these two halves make one nation. Lazarus's apprentice-
ship finally achieves here a powerful blending of the conventional
device of alliteration, melodramatic declaration, true feeling, and
sincere expression. Gone is the adjective-hunting Lazarus lived by in
former versifying;[16] gone are the trite images and posed emotions.
Simplicity carries its own power.

The "priest and mob" come in for more powerful castigation in
"The Crowing of the Red Cock." The "red cock" was the peasant's
code-image of an anti-Jewish pogrom in Russia. In a paroxysm of
irony, she points out that Christianity is destroying the people of
which its own God was a member and is, indeed, violating His
teaching:

> Where is the Hebrew's fatherland?
> The folk of Christ is sore bestead;
> The Son of Man is bruised and banned,
> Nor finds whereon to lay his head.
> His cup is gall, his meat is tears.
> His passion lasts a thousand years.
>
> When the long roll of Christian guilt
> Against his sires and him is known,
> The flood of tears, the life-blood spilt,
> The agony of ages shown,
> What oceans can the stain remove,
> From Christian law and Christian love?
>
> *(Poems*, II, 3-4)

John Greenleaf Whittier thought this "forceful lyric worthy of the
Maccabean age." [17]

Whittier's allusion to the Maccabean age, when the five sons of
Mattathias Maccabeus led the successful revolt against the Syrian
Greeks in 168 B. C., came from another poem in *Songs of a Semite*,
perhaps the most powerful thing in it, "The Banner of the Jew."
Here, the atonement for "In The Jewish Synagogue of Newport" is
finally completed. Here, Emma Lazarus calls for, believes in, and
evokes the renaissance of the Jewish nation:

THE BANNER OF THE JEW

> Wake, Israel, wake! Recall to-day
> The glorious Maccabean rage,

The sire heroic, hoary-gray,
    His five-fold lion-lineage:
The Wise, the Elect, the Help–of–God,
The Burst–of–Spring, the Avenging Rod.

From Mizpeh's mountain–ridge they saw
    Jerusalem's empty streets, her shrine
Laid waste where Greeks profaned the Law,
    With idol and with pagan sign.
Mourners in tattered black were there,
With ashes sprinkled on their hair.

Then from the stony peak there rang
    A blast to ope the graves: down poured
The Maccabean clan, who sang
    Their battle–anthem to the Lord.
Five heroes lead, and following, see,
Ten thousand rush to victory!

Oh for Jerusalem's trumpet now,
    To blow a blast of shattering power,
To wake the sleepers high and low,
    And rouse them to the urgent hour!
No hand for vengeance—but to save,
A million naked swords should wave.

O deem not dead that martial fire,
    Say not the mystic flame is spent!
With Moses' law and David's lyre,
    Your ancient strength remains unbent.
Let but an Ezra rise anew,
To lift the *Banner of the Jew*!

A rag, a mock at first—erelong,
    When men have bled and women wept,
To guard its precious folds from wrong,
    Even they who shrunk, even they who slept,
Shall leap to bless it, and to save.
Strike! for the brave revere the brave!

                              (*Poems*, II, 10–12; Lazarus's italics)

The law-giver, the God-intoxicated bard, and the teacher are all
traditional heroes in the Jewish pantheon, but for Lazarus in the grip
of her anger, the fighter is greater than they. No longer the genteel
Victorian lady scribbler, Emma Lazarus astonished the *Century*

critic into observing, "Strange that it should be a woman to say that word: 'Strike! for the brave revere the brave.' " [18]

In these poems, Lazarus's most potent instruments are alliteration and periodic declamation, not imagery or quaint turns of phrase. Periods like, "His cup is gall / his meat is tears / His passion lasts a thousand years" is in the rhetorical tradition of using incremental repetition and irony in tandem. It is Ciceronian prose applied to poetry.

The most peaceful poem in the collection is one called "In Exile," an imaginative description of the twilight of a day in the life of a Russian Jewish family that followed the sun to a farm in Texas. One of the refugees had written a letter to the *Jewish Messenger* (April 28, 1882) describing what happens on the new farm when day is done: "Every evening after supper we take a seat under the mighty oak and sing our songs." (Lazarus did not know it, but at just about this time, the other stream of Jewry of which she spoke, the one which flowed east to Palestine, began to till the ancient land in what was to become the *kibbutz* movement, and they too, at evening, sat under the trees to sing songs.)

The scene inspired Emma Lazarus. Characteristically, she begins derivatively, echoing the most famous of all eventide poems, Gray's "Elegy Written in a Country Churchyard":

> Twilight is here, soft breezes bow the grass,
>   Day's sounds of various toil breaks slowly off.
> The yoke-freed oxen low, the patient ass
>   Dips his dry nostril in the cool, deep trough.
> Up from the prairie the tanned herdsmen pass.

Gray's idealized rustics here become

> Strange faces . . . wherethrough the Orient sun
>   Gleams from the eye and glows athwart
>   the skin.
> Grave lines of studious thought and purpose run
>   From curl-crowned forehead to dark-bearded chin[19]. . .
> In fire and blood through ages on their name,
> Their seal of glory and the Gentiles' shame.
>
> > (*Poems*, II, 5–6)

It took a great deal of effort for this daughter of aristocratic, Americanized, German-Sephardi Jews, reared in an atmosphere of modernity and sophisticated culture, to feel emotional kinship with these strange Russian Jews, to feel an anger controlled only by the serenity of the scene the poem depicts.

The history of literature is replete with poets whom wars, rebellions, even politics, inspired to moments of greatness. Lazarus is one of them. As the *Century's* critic went on to say—

Miss Emma Lazarus of New York, after writing prose and verse of a high grade on topics having to do with anything but Hebrew matters, has recently developed in a line which cannot help exciting the finest indignation of which she is capable, and which in fact has called out her very best resources. Her success hitherto, has been among Christians rather than her own folk, but now she appeals to her race.[20]

It is these poems, and those in the same vein which she wrote in the next few years that carried her name into the history of American literature for the ensuing half-century. We need only to recall Van Wyck Brooks's comment: "How far a cause could vitalize and magnify a talent one saw in the case of . . . the Jewess Emma Lazarus." [21]

CHAPTER 13

Last Songs of the Semite

I   Residual Anger and Momentary Peace

WHATEVER else *Songs of a Semite* might have been, it was no cathartic for Emma Lazarus. The anger and bitter irony that characterized those songs were not assuaged. Her emotions found their way into poems that immediately followed upon the appearance of that book. "The World's Justice" (November 1882), and "The Supreme Sacrifice" (May 1884) sound similar themes of persecution and the world's indifference. The counterpart vision of resurrected Hebrew heroism is again announced in "The Feast of Lights [Hannukah]" (December 1882), which amplifies the call for a Maccabean hero, and in "Bar Kochba," a sonnet celebrating the hero of the Jewish revolt against Rome in A.D. 132, "the last warrior Jew" [1] (*Poems*, II, 22). Resurrection and Return are themes combined in "The New Ezekiel," where she uses the prophet's parable of the dry bones inspirited with life by God to express His promise to "place you living in your land" (*Poems*, II, 15). These are strong, competent lyrics, but no more strong or competent than the others already published.

For one moment, Lazarus found a respite from these volcanic themes in the one translation from medieval Hebrew poetry that she rendered directly from the original Hebrew. No translation from the French of her beloved Hugo, or from the German of her admired Goethe and Heine, or from the Italian of her respected Petrarch called forth such an expression of pride as—

It is from some Spanish Hebrew poet, but I am sorry to say I do not know which one. [It was Alcharisi.] I have translated this from the original Hebrew—& so am very proud of it as my first effort! [2]

CONSOLATION

Oh were my streaming tears to flow,
According to my grievous woe,
Then foot of man in all his quest
On no dry spot of earth could rest.
But not to Noah's flood alone,
The Covenant's bright pledge was shown,
For likewise to my tears and woe
Behold once more revealed the Bow! [3]

This is nearly a metaphysical conceit. The exaggeration of the first four lines is just the kind of thing John Donne liked to do to poetize the flow of tears. And he too used the analogy to Noah's flood that logically rises from the image of the earth inundated by tears. The allusion to Noah's rainbow, the sign of God's covenant with man never again to destroy him by a flood, is at once cosmological and personal. For it is also the sign of God's consolation for one who is sorrowed that the tears will eventually cease and life will be revived.

As usual, her translation is in spirit, not literal. It had to be: Hebrew is much more telegraphic and idiomatic than the European languages she was used to. It is not to be believed that she mastered Hebrew. The best that can be said is that she came to know the language well enough to understand Alcharisi's intentions and imagery. Alcharisi's little poem perhaps also had the sentimental value of being a kind of gloss on "Links," the tiny lyric of 1866 in which Lazarus, too, had condensed the chain of being into one spiritual image that reached the heavens.

This seems to have been the only translation of a Jewish poem in this period. Petrarch claimed her interest intermittently between 1881 and 1884, not only the Sonnets of *In Vita di Madonna Laura*, but also the sonnets and canzone of *In Morte di Madonna Laura*. [4] But her mind could not persist in dealing with themes of love, or even of lovelorn death, as in her days of yore. More momentous themes of sadness claimed her.

II   *Contemporary Lamentations*

In October 1883, Lazarus wrote a series of what she called "Little Poems in Prose" and entitled them "By the Waters of Babylon." (They were not published until 1887.) In them, Lazarus strikes a poetic note unique in her entire canon. Influenced perhaps by the

Psalms and prophetic poetry of the King James Version of the Bible (and by Walt Whitman, according to Zeiger),[5] she tried free verse for the first and only time. In a sense, the attempt was an outgrowth of a widening appreciation of the Bible as a work of literature and maybe of a final intuitive recognition of the value of her own blank verse. We must conclude, however, that either she did not understand the principles of biblical verse in English or of Whitman's verse, or she developed a different idea of free verse for herself.

Here are three passages from "I. Exodus (August 3, 1492)":

2.   The hoary patriarch, wrinkled as an almond shell, bows painfully upon his staff. The beautiful young mother, ivory pale, well-nigh swoons beneath her burden; in her large enfolding arms nestles her sleeping babe, round her knees flock her little ones with bruised and bleeding feet. "Mother, shall we soon be there?"

9.   Woe to the straggler who falls by the wayside! No friend shall close his eyes.

10.   They leave behind, the grape, the olive, and the fig; the vines they planted, the corn they sowed, the garden cities of Andalusia and Aragon, Estramadura and La Mancha, of Granada and Castile; the altar, the hearth, and the grave of their fathers.   (*Poems*, II, 58–59)

In the main, free verse to Emma Lazarus was a series of facts overlaid with a veneer of sentimentality. Though she uses parallelism, notably in verse 10, it is of the kind that worked more successfully in her prose. Her periodic clauses, syntactically parallel, build into a compendium rather than into a structure of cadence and climax. She shows no real concept of the unrhymed parallelisms upon which the poetry of the King James Version is built and by which Whitman channeled his lines, catalogs, and cadences. That she was not the only one who misunderstood how unfree the new free verse really was is evidenced by the comment one critic made about the form of "By the Waters of Babylon:" "Truly poetry in prose which indicates the lines upon which her poetic power would have developed." [6]

Thematically, "By the Waters of Babylon" is a recapitulation of all the themes she had written about the last few years. She reviews the millennia of the Jewish exile. She bewails the covering of the "diamond," the symbol of Israel, but rejoices in the imminent uncovering of Truth, "the delicate pearl," and of the Law, the "adamantine jewel" (*Poems*, II, 60–61). Irony underlies the stanzas called "The Sower," wherein Lazarus pictures Israel dropping "fecund seeds" that become Christianity and Islam, which turn on the Sower and betray both their origins and their own beauties (*Poems*, II, pp. 61–62).

A controversial element in these "poems" is her treatment of ghetto-seared Jews, the kind she saw come from Eastern Europe, those in her descriptions of "the shuffling gait, the ignominious features, the sordid mask of the son of the Ghetto" (*Poems*, II, 63). When two years earlier she first essayed this picture in "Epistle to the Hebrews", she was scolded in letters to the editor and she backtracked. But she simply could not reconcile these meek Jews with her ideal poets and heroes of the Hebrew past.

Her final image is of the "Soul of Israel burst[ing] her cobweb sheath" by virtue of the "wholesome, quickening airs" of Emancipation, "fly[ing] forth attired in the winged beauty of immortality" (*Poems*, II, 66–67). She may not have loved every Jew, but in her poetry she showed that she loved the people.

III   *Final Lamentation*

In May 1884,[7] Lazarus wrote one of her finest sonnets, "Venus of the Louvre," inspired during a quick visit to Paris in July 1883 from her base in London.[8] Anyone whoever breathlessly hurried down the corridor leading to the rotunda where the Venus stands will appreciate Lazarus's opening lines:

VENUS OF THE LOUVRE

> Down the long hall she glistens like a star,
> The foam-born mother of Love, transfixed to stone,
> Yet none the less immortal, breathing on.
> Time's brutal hand hath maimed but could not mar.
> When first the enthralled enchantress from afar
> Dazzled mine eyes, I saw not her alone,
> Serenely poised on her world-worshipped throne,
> As when she guided once her dove-drawn car,—
> But at her feet a pale, death–stricken Jew,
> Her life adorer, sobbed farewell to love.
> Here *Heine* wept! Here still he weeps anew,
> Nor ever shall his shadow lift or move,
> While mourns one ardent heart, one poet-brain,
> For vanished Hellas and Hebraic pain.

(Poems, I, 203)

This is a sonnet of discovery, of wonder, like Keats' sonnet on discovering Chapman's Homer. In the octet, she pays tribute to the statue, declaring that mutilation may maim "but could not mar" the sculpture. But Lazarus was inspired by quite another theme as well. In a striking use of the Petrarchan shift in line 9 of a sonnet, she suddenly introduces the "death–stricken Jew," Heine. And Lazarus identified with him more closely than ever before. She, like Heine, had come home from a long spiritual exile. In her, as in Heine—

> . . . mourns one ardent heart, one poet-brain,
> For vanished Hellas and Hebraic pain.

She did not know at that moment that she, too, was to become mortally and painfully ill. Josephine Lazarus, in her memoir, recalls that Emma in Paris in 1887 enacted the same tableau as the sonnet describes:

Once again came the analogy, which [Emma] herself pointed out now, to Heine on his mattress-grave in Paris. She, too, the last time she went out, dragged herself to the Louvre, to the feet of the Venus, "the goddess without arms, who could not help." (*Poems*, I, 36)

IV   *Long-glittering Words*

There's an interesting anecdote that tells how Emma Lazarus's most famous poem, the Statue of Liberty sonnet, came to be. By the fall of 1883, Bartholdi's statue of the lady with the torch had been delivered and awaited erection. The U.S. Congress agreed to allocate a sum to help erect the statue, but *not* the pedestal! Public-spirited citizens thereupon formed a committee, and one of their fund-raising projects was a Bartholdi Statue Pedestal Art Loan Exhibition to be held on December 3, 1883. As part of the project, famous authors were to be asked to write something appropriate and to allow the manuscript of their offering to be auctioned. So a committee member asked the popular Emma Lazarus:

She was at first inclined to rebel against writing "anything to order" as it were, the story goes, and rather mischievously let play the summer-lighting of her sarcasm upon her [visitor]. . . . When reminded of Russian refugees as recipients of the light of the torch, her dark eyes deepened—her cheek flushed—the time for merriment was passed—she said not a word more, then.[9]

Apparently, Lazarus intuited an historic opportunity here, because, before she settled on the text of "The New Colossus," she tried out the theme and some imagery in two other, less satisfactory, poems. One was a sonnet entitled "1492," dated in the manuscript notebook December 1883. 1492 was a "two-faced year," which saw both exile and

> . . . A virgin world where door of sunset part,
> Saying, "Ho, all who weary, enter here! . . ."
>
> *(Poems, II, 23)*

The last words would echo in "The New Colossus." The other poem is entitled "Gifts," also dated in manuscript 1883 (not published until 1885). Here Lazarus imagines the Egyptian of the ancient world asking the "World God" for wealth, and getting it, but now "Rust and the moth, silence and dusty sleep" mark that civilization. The Greek asked for beauty: "Today / A broken column and a lute unstrung" are all that is left. The Roman got "Power," but "a roofless ruin stands where once abode / The imperial race of everlasting Rome." The Hebrew, however, requested "Truth," was exiled, but remains "Immortal through the lamp within his hand" *(Poems,* II, pp. 20–21).

From the fusion of theme, expression, and images in these poems arose:

THE NEW COLOSSUS

> Not like the brazen giant of Greek fame
> With conquering limbs astride from land to land;
> Here at our sea-washed, sunset gates shall stand
> A mighty woman with a torch, whose flame
> Is the imprisoned lightning, and her name
> Mother of Exiles. From her beacon-hand
> Glows world-wide welcome; her mild eyes command
> The air-bridged harbor that twin cities frame,
> "Keep, ancient lands, your storied pomp!" cries she
> With silent lips, "Give me your tired, your poor,
> Your huddled masses yearning to breathe free,
> The wretched refuse of your teeming shore,
> Send these, the homeless, tempest-tost to me,
> I lift my lamp beside the golden door!"
>
> *(Poems, I, 202–03)*

The poem was read at the auction on December 3; it was recited at the dedication of the statue on October 28, 1886; it is enshrined on a plaque in the pedestal of the Statue; and, now that immigrants arrive by flying over the Statue, the last four and a half lines are engraved into the wall of the Reception Hall of New York International Airport. Comment on the sonnet seems superfluous, but something must be said nevertheless.

Some of Lazarus's old poetic habits—alliteration, newly-coined hyphenated adjectives, and pure sentiment—are present, and the sophisticated ear of Wolcott Gibbs years later led him to remark, "[This sonnet] may easily be the most lamentable collection of words ever thus preserved for the ages." [10] But only two weeks after the sonnet was first recited, James Russell Lowell, himself no mean literary critic, saw in "The New Colossus" the making of an immortal poem:

I must write again to say how much I like your sonnet about the Statue— much better than I like the Statue itself. But your sonnet gives its subject a *raison d'etre* which it wanted before quite as much as it wants a pedestal. You have set it on a noble one, saying admirably just the right word to be said, an achievement more arduous than that of the sculptor. I have just been writing a sonnet myself & know how difficult material one had to work in—how much more difficult when the subject is prescribed & not chosen. [11]

Despite its faults, "The New Colossus" has become part of the living voice of America.

"The New Colossus" represents a summary and a climax of Emma Lazarus's lifelong literary endeavors. She too had begun by worshiping at the Greek shrine, a cultural inheritance that dominated her as the Colossus dominated the waterway into Rhodes. But, in time, an earthquake of an emotional and ethnic origin destroyed that shrine. The culture it represented, "the storied pomp," had been rejected. In its place, pride in America's welcome to the oppressed and in the persistence of her own Jewish people now demanded celebration and received it in this poem of affirmation that popular America took to its heart. It is not too much to say that the sonnet can stand as a kind of allegory of a literary spirit that itself yearned to breathe free but did not know how, and finally learned what freedom really is. Freedom is coming home.

CHAPTER 14

The Lazarus Legacy

IN 1882 an unwittingly symbolic meeting took place between
Emma Lazarus and Abraham Cahan, a newly arrived Russian-
Jewish immigrant. In his autobiography Cahan recalls the incident:

> When I arrived the immigration committee included one wealthy young
> Jewish lady who belonged to the cream of the monied aristocracy. She was
> Emma Lazarus. She often visited the immigrants' camp on Ward's Island in
> the East River, but this never undermined her status as an aristocrat.
>   She was of the Portuguese Jews, the oldest Jewish families in
> America. . . .[1]

Thus the author of *Songs of a Semite* symbolically passed on the torch
to the future author of *The Rise of David Levinsky* (1917), the arche-
typal novel about a Russian-Jewish immigrant from which all future
American-Jewish fiction derived themes and techniques.[2]

Historically speaking, we may say that the meeting presaged the
imminent shift of dominance from the old Portuguese-German Jewish class to the new, rough, unmolded Russian-Jewish group. The
latter brought with it a highly developed but terribly monolithic
intellectualism that had just now begun the process of emancipation
in Europe. This intellectualism was still circumscribed by strict
religion, but those walls were about to be tumbled by the shock of
emancipation. From this shock and from this group would arise
Cahan's fiction and the fiction of American Jews down to the present,
all of them descendants of East European transplanted Jewry, all of
them still groping in a world partially encompassed by the mentality
of the *shtetl*, the East European Jewish town.

The legacy that they received upon entering the world of letters,
beside all of the other cultural and literary influences, is the legacy of
Emma Lazarus. First, she left them a consciousness of the importance of their Jewish heritage as a point of departure for their fiction
and poetry. Though her early writings avoided Jewish topics to

celebrate a general kind of cultural humanism, she came to learn that writing about Jews means writing about all humanity. As Leslie Fiedler has pointed out, the Jew is the mythic American[3] in the works of Saul Bellow, Bernard Malamud, and Philip Roth. On a more universal plane, Lazarus stripped the suffering Christian God of his narrow theology and made him into a Jewish symbol of suffering, and thus presaged the symbolism of Edward Lewis Wallant's novels and even of Chaim Potok's *My Name Is Asher Lev*. And in her very life are the germs of so many novels of attempted assimilation and the ultimate rejection of it.

Secondly, she left to her literary progeny an American public prepared and willing to accept the writings of American Jews and other Americans from minority groups. The encouragement of Emerson and Stedman presaged the encouragement William Dean Howells gave to Abraham Cahan, and that in turn anticipated the phenomenal popular and critical acclaim of American-Jewish writing after World War II. The conditioning of the American public to interest itself in—indeed, to *see* itself in—the troubles and victories of the Jew began with Emma Lazarus's essays and poems.

On the other hand, the shift from the genre of poetry to the genre of fiction symbolizes the gap between the genteel Romanticism of Lazarus and the humanistic Realism of those who followed her. For all the immediacy and anger of Lazarus's Jewish poems, her vision of heroism is apt for an age of innocence. She was a Romantic who hoped for a Maccabean Byron to rise and fight the dragons enslaving her people.

It is a concept out of step with our generation of American Jewish writers of fiction. Except for the later Saul Bellow and Meyer Levin, most see heroism in mere endurance. If the schlemihl can survive, he has achieved victory. Ironically, this is precisely the picture Lazarus conjured up in her private mind before 1880, and for which she begged forgiveness in later letters and essays. No, her kind of hero is not found in today's fiction.

To find a closer literary inheritance pertaining to Jewish heroism, we must turn to American Jewish poetry. Muriel Rukeyser, Linda Pasten, Charles Reznikoff, Karl Shapiro, and Hyam Plutzik are some who had the courage of an Emma Lazarus to declare that the Jew is more than a schlemiel. They are impressed with his persistence throughout the Exile, with his irrefrangible clutching at a meaningful, creative future. They, like Lazarus, write poems of indignation, pride, and hope. In their work there is no resignation to mere

survival. Heroism resounds through their verse because the cadences of the Bible and the medieval visionaries are heard there as in
Lazarus's verse. But the genre of poetry is today distinctly minor
compared to the fiction.

As a poetic stylist, if her poetry will receive further study, Emma
Lazarus will not be served by acolytes of John Donne and T. S. Eliot.
Her images are not metaphysical; her paradoxes are not clever. She is
devoid of ambiguities. A comparison with Emily Dickinson for technique or with Robert Frost for covert complexity would simply be
fruitless. She belongs in that special section of the Poets' Valhalla
reserved for those who are beloved more than studied, like Longfellow, Whittier, Sandburg, E. A. Robinson. With them, she is the
spokesman, not of the head, but of the heart, where, in addition to
love, courage resides.

Notes and References

Preface

1. Alfred Kazin, "The Jew as Modern Writer," *Commentary*, 41 (April 1966), 37.
2. E. C. Stedman in the *American Hebrew Memorial Issue*, December 9, 1887, p. 4.
3. George F. Whicher, "Poetry after the Civil War," in *American Writers on Literature*, ed. John Macy (New York, 1931), p. 382.

Chapter One

1. Hyman B. Grinstein, *The Rise of the Jewish Community of New York, 1654–1860* (Philadelphia, 1947), p. 169.
2. E. R. Ellis, *The Epic of New York* (New York, 1966), pp. 248, 257.
3. Philip Cowen, "Emma Lazarus," repr. in *Autobiographies of American Jews*, ed. Harold U. Ribalow (Philadelphia, 1968), p. 33.
4. David de Sola Pool, *An Old Faith in a New World: A Portrait of Shearith Israel* (New York, 1955), pp. 174, 178, 85.
5. "An Epistle to the Hebrews," *American Hebrew*, February 9, 1883, p. 149.
6. Josephine Lazarus, "Emma Lazarus," in *The Poems of Emma Lazarus* (Boston, 1889), I, p. 7. Hereafter this collection will be referred to as *Poems*, and quotations will be based wherever possible on this edition.
7. Geraldine Rosenfeld, "Emma Lazarus and Heinrich Heine," unpubl. master's thesis, Columbia University, New York, 1939, p. 3.
8. Morris U. Schappes, ed., *The Letters of Emma Lazarus, 1868–1885* (New York, 1949), p. 7. Hereafter this volume will be referred to as *E. L. Letters*.
9. The basic motif of W. E. Jacob, *The World of Emma Lazarus* (New York, 1949).
10. *E. L. Letters*, p. 18.
11. Ralph. L. Rusk, ed., *Letters to Emma Lazarus in the Columbia University Library* (New York, 1939), p. 25. Hereafter this collection will be referred to as *Letters to E. L.*
12. May 9, 1878; *Letters to E. L.*, p. 25.
13. January 17, 1885; *Letters to E. L.*, p. 28.

14. *American Hebrew Memorial Issue*, p. 6.

15. To Rabbi Gustav Gottheil, February 6, 1877; *E. L. Letters*, pp. 19–20.

16. Quoted by Kazin, "Jew as Modern Writer," p. 37.

17. *American Hebrew Memorial Issue*, p. 4.

18. Mark Wischnitzer, *To Dwell in Safety* (Philadelphia, 1948), pp. 40, 51.

19. Richard Gottheil, *Life of Gustav Gottheil* (Williamsport, Pa., 1936), p. 61.

20. "An Epistle to the Hebrews," *American Hebrew*, November 17, 1882, p. 4.

21. "The Schiff Refuge," *American Hebrew*, October 27, 1882, p. 125.

22. See Albert Mordell (who quotes Schappes), "Some Final Words on Emma Lazarus," *Publications of the American Jewish Historical Society*, 39 (1950), 324–25.

23. Gottheil, p. 64; "Emma Lazarus," *American Hebrew*, November 25, 1887, p. 35.

24. Gustav Karpeles, *Jewish Literature and Other Essays* (Philadelphia, 1895), pp. 140–41.

25. See *E. L. Letters* and *Letters to E. L.* for 1883.

26. Quoted by Arthur Zeiger, "Emma Lazarus: A Critical Study," unpublished doctoral dissertation, New York University, 1951, p. 170, n. 272. My debt to this study, though often in disagreement, is reflected in my many references to "Zeiger."

27. *New York Times*, November 22, 1887, p. 5. A case has been made for Lazarus's "conversion" to Ethical Culture, based on a reported visit to her deathbed by its founder, Dr. Felix Adler. But the same account reports her request for burial according to Orthodox Jewish ritual, a factor which casts some doubt on the depth of the conversion. See Zeiger, pp. 169, 181.

28. Clipping in present author's possession; place of original publication unknown.

29. Horace Traubel, *With Walt Whitman in Camden* (New York, 1908; repr., ed. Sculley Bradley, 1953), II, 456, 459.

30. Quoted in *American Hebrew*, April 19, 1889, p. 182.

31. One demurring voice was Ludwig Lewisohn's. He found her sonnets "pseudo-noble," "conventional," "not of silver, but of tin." Quoted by Alfred Werner, "An American Deborah," *Contemporary Jewish Record* (1945), 88.

32. *Letters to E. L.*, p. v.

Chapter Two

1. This volume (hereafter referred to as *Poems and Translations*) was privately printed in 1866. In 1867, Hurd and Houghton of Boston brought out an edition apparently from the same plates but with additional poems. The latest poem in the 1866 edition is "Daphne," February 12, 1866. "Recollections of Shakespeare," added in the later edition, is dated June 4, 1866.

2. Quoted by J. C. Wilson, *American Hebrew Memorial Issue*, p. 3. The

age Bryant mentions is, of course, wrong.

3. William James to Emma Lazarus, August 26, 1882; *Letters to E. L.*, p. 48.

4. Gladys Graham, "Lazarus, Emma," *Dictionary of American Biography*, XI, p. 65.

5. Zieger, p. 2.

6. Zieger, p. 2. Zieger also nominates Poe's "A Dream within a Dream" as the source of Lazarus's "Only a Dream." However, a close reading of both reveals that the analogue is the *1827 version* of Poe's poem, not the later printed versions. It is doubtful that Lazarus found the 1827 version to read.

7. Yvor Winters, "Edgar Allan Poe: A Crisis in the History of American Obscurantism," repr. *In Defense of Reason* (New York, 1947), p. 259.

8. *New York Times*, February 23, 1867, p. 2.

9. Zieger, p. 7., n. 16. His list of poems influenced by Tennyson (p. 3) includes the romances as well as five lyrics.

10. Rosenfeld, p. 20.

11. *Ibid.*, p. 17.

12. See Charles Feidelson, Jr., *Symbolism and American Literature* (1953; repr. Chicago, 1970), p. 123.

13. "The Poet" (1844) in *Selections from Ralph Waldo Emerson*, ed. Stephen E. Whicher (Boston, 1957), p. 232–33.

14. Josephine Lazarus (*Poems*, I, 2) recalls that Emma "was eleven years old when the War of the Secession broke out, . . . which inspired her first lyric outbursts." These juvenilia are apparently lost.

15. "Booth, John Wilkes," *Encyclopedia Americana* (1972), IV, 262; see also Jim Bishop, *The Day Lincoln Was Shot* (New York, 1956), p. 294.

16. Zieger, p. 3.

17. *New York Times*, February 23, 1867, p. 2.

18. *Letters to E. L.*, pp. 3–4.

19. *Ibid.*

Chapter Three

1. *Letters to E. L.*, p. 4.

2. *Ibid.*

3. June 23, 1868; *Letters to E. L.*, p. 7.

4. *Letters of Ralph Waldo Emerson*, ed. Ralph L. Rusk (New York, 1939), VI, 14.

5. June 27, 1868; *E. L. Letters*, p. 7.

6. August 24, 1868; *E. L. Letters*, p. 8.

7. *Letters to E. L.*, pp. 9–10.

8. *Ibid.*, p. 9.

9. *Ibid.*, p. 9.

10. July 9, 1869; *Letters to E. L.*, p. 12.

11. Originally in *Admetus*, pp. 182–85. Max I. Baym, "Emma Lazarus and

Emerson," *Publications of American Jewish Historical Society*, 38 (1949), p. 267, says this poem marks Lazarus's "mental journey from Greece to America." Not so. "Heroes" is simultaneous with "Admetus" and "Orpheus"; it predates "Lohengrin" and "Tannhauser," That journey comes later.

12. June 7, 1869; *Letters to E. L.*, p. 11. Emerson remarked that "Mr. [James Russell] Lowell is right" regarding the poem's weaknesses. How Lowell came to see the poem is not clear: either Lazarus or Emerson offered it to him for the *North American Review*.

13. *Letters to E. L.*, p. 14.

14. *Letters to E. L.*, pp. 15–16.

15. *E. L. Letters*, p. 13.

16. *E. L. Letters*, p. 12.

17. See Baym, "Emma Lazarus and Emerson," p. 278, and Mordell, "Final Words," p. 324.

18. *Letters of Emerson*, VI, 296, n. 21.

19. Ralph L. Rusk, *Life of Ralph Waldo Emerson* (New York, 1949), p. 494.

20. "Emerson's Personality," *Century*, 24 (July 1882), 455–56.

21. "To R. W. E.," *Critic*, 4 (August 1884), 5–6.

Chapter Four

1. *Admetus and Other Poems* (New York and Boston, 1871).

2. October 2, 1869; *Letters of Emerson*, VI, 90, n. 148.

3. J. W. Mackail, *The Life of William Morris* (London, 1920), I, 193, 196.

4. Zeiger's analysis of the differences, pp. 10–12, in several ways comports with mine. However, I do not agree with his conclusion that "Admetus" comes off poorly in the comparison.

5. *The Earthly Paradise* (London, 1890), pp. 128–40.

6. *Illustrated London News*, October 14, 1871, p. 359.

7. *Westminster Review*, 190 (1871), 271. The title of the book given at the head of this review is, unaccountably, " 'Adventures and other Poems' by Emma Lazarus."

8. Zeiger, p. 15.

9. Rosenfeld reads "Tannhäuser" as a shift of emphasis in Lazarus "to a nineteenth century American transcendental expression against ceremonial and creed"; "Lazarus and Heine," p. 21.

10. Zeiger, p. 17.

11. *Galaxy*, 19 (January 1872), p. 136.

12. *Nation*, February 12, 1872, p. 92.

13. *Lippincott's*, 8 (November 1871), 526–27.

14. Albert Mordell, "Some Neglected Phases of Emma Lazarus' Genius," *Jewish Forum*, 39 (October 1949), 181.

15. Stephen Birmingham, *The Grandees* (New York, 1971), p. 277. In the book, "family sources" are cited. In a letter to me, Mr. Birmingham identifies

these sources as "personal interviews with descendants." No further corrob-
oration of either Mordell or Birmingham has come to light.

16. Zeiger, pp. 25, 28; see *Letters to E. L.*, p. 15.
17. Mordell, "Some Neglected Phases . . . ", p. 181.
18. Zeiger, p. 29.
19. *Letters of Emerson*, VI, 21, n. 84.
20. Zeiger, p. 22.

Chapter Five

1. Zeiger, p. 188.
2. *Letters to E. L.*, p. 18.
3. *E. L. Letters*, p. 16.
4. *E. L. Letters*, p. 19.
5. Zeiger, p. 209.
6. *Poems*, I, 16.
7. *Poems*, I, 15.
8. Louis Ruchames, "New Light on the Religious Development of Emma
Lazarus," *Publications of the American Jewish Historical Society*, 42 (1952),
83. The poem is reprinted on pp. 86–8.
9. *Ibid.*, p. 85.
10. *Ibid.*, pp. 86–88.
11. *Ibid.*, p. 88.

Chapter Six

1. Zeiger, p. 193, reads the manuuuscript as "thy shy moonbeams[']
dance" (brackets his). My close study of the manuscript photostats convinces
me that Lazarus never forgot a punctuation mark and that her "d" 's do not
resemble her "s" 's. My reading places the bliss where Miss Lazarus would
place erotic pleasure—in the dark. The poem appears on leaf 19.
2. Zeiger, p. 192.
3. *Encyclopaedia Britannica*, 14th ed. (1929), pp. 108–09.
4. *Poems*, I, 201.
5. *Poems*, I, 219–20.
6. The sonnet was printed in the *New York Times*, October 2, 1881, p. 2.
The exchange of letters with George is in *E. L. Letters*, pp. 31–33, together
with *Letters to E. L.*, pp. 34–35.
7. *Collier's Encyclopedia* (1961), IX, 696.
8. *Century*, 25 (December 1879), 196.

Chapter Seven

1. "Eugene Fromentin," *Critic*, 1 (December 1881), 364.
2. *Ibid.*

3. Zeiger, p. 217, n. 94.

4. *Lippincott's*, 13 (June 1874), 774.

5. *Alide: An Episode in Goethe's Life* (Philadelphia, 1874), pp. 11–12. Further citations are provided in parentheses in the text.

6. *Lippincott's*, 13 (June 1874), 775.

7. Zeiger, p. 218.

8. Quoted in advertisement for *Alide* in *American Hebrew*, September 22, 1882, p. 73.

9. *Lippincott's*, 13 (June 1874), 775.

10. *Jewish Messenger*, April 17, 1874, p. 5.

11. Morris U. Schappes, ed., *Emma Lazarus: Selections from Her Poetry and Prose* (New York, 1944), p. 10.

12. September 2, 1874; *Letters to E. L.*, p. 17.

13. Zeiger, p. 224.

14. *Century*, 16 (June 1878), 242–56.

15. *Poems*, I, 33.

Chapter Eight

1. *Selections from Emerson*, p. 238.

2. *E. L. Letters*, p. 67, n. 72b. *The Poets of America* was published in 1885.

3. *E. L. Letters*, pp. 67–68. Schappes thinks that Stedman's later theory of the Genius as the counterbalance to adverse conditions for art in a society was influenced by Lazarus's letter.

4. *Critic*, 1 (June 1881), 164, published anonymously. Lazarus is identified as the author in a letter to Higginson in which she acknowledges receipt of his "Memorial Ode" that he had sent "to the author of the article in the Critic of June 18th on American literature"; *E. L. Letters*, p. 29. Woodberry's article had appeared in the *Fortnightly Review*; references to it here are from Lazarus's essay.

5. *Ibid.*

6. "Joseffy," *Musical Review*, 1 (November 16, 1879), p. 52.

7. *Ibid.*

8. "In Southern Europe," *Jewish Messenger*, June 25, 1880, pp. 4–5.

9. The manuscript notebook has a clipped printed version of this poem on leaves 120 and 121. In May 1875 Lazarus had written "On the Proposal to Erect a Monument in England to Lord Byron." She recounts the glory of his death at Missolonghi, Greece, and scores the refusal to allow a monument in Westminster Abbey. Byron, she says, does not really need the memorial, but England does in order to erase the blot of not recognizing Byron's genius. See Samuel C. Chew, *Byron in England* (London, 1924), pp. 294–95.

10. Gordon S. Haight, "Realism Defined: William Dean Howells," in *Literary History of the United States*, (New York, 1948) II, 878. See also Lars Ähnebrink, *The Beginnings of Naturalism in America* (Uppsalla, 1950), pp. 28–29.

11. "Bernay as 'Marc Antony'," *Century*, 26 (June 1883), 312.

12. "A Day in Surrey with William Morris," *Century*, 32 (July 1886), 388, 395. Interestingly, there is no mention of the disclaimer in *Admetus and Other Poems* that she plagiarized *The Earthly Paradise*.

13. *Ibid.*, pp. 395–96.

Chapter Nine

1. Published in 1881 by R. Worthington; reprinted New York: Hartsdale House, 1947. The latter edition is the one cited here.

2. Rosenfeld, p. 18.

3. Frederick Ewen, ed., *Poetry and Prose of Heinrich Heine* (New York, 1948), p. 16.

4. H. B. Sachs, *Heine in America* (Philadelphia, 1916), p. 117.

5. *Poems*, I, 17.

6. Aaron Kramer, "The Link between Heinrich Heine and Emma Lazarus" (New York [bound reprint from *Publications of the American Jewish Historical Society*], 1956), p. 253.

7. *E. L. Letters*, p. 29.

8. Kramer, p. 252.

9. In a letter to Moses Moser, November 5 or 6, 1823; *Gesammelte Wërke* (Hamburg, 1861), vol. 19, p. 125.

10. Quoted in *American Hebrew*, December 17, 1882, p. 4.

11. *Critic*, 1 (June 1881), 163.

12. Sachs, p. 188.

13. Zeiger, p. 61.

14. *Critic*, 1 (June 1881), 163.

15. "Miss Lazarus's Translation of Heine," *Century*, 23 (March 1882), 785–86. See Rosenfeld, pp. 51ff.

16. *New York Times*, July 10, 1881, p. 10.

17. Sachs, p. 117.

18. Mordell, "Some Neglected Phases of Emma Lazarus' Genius," p. 182.

19. Rosenfeld, p. 33.

20. Introduction, *Poems and Ballads*, pp. 9–10, 14, 15.

21. *Ibid.*, p. 15.

22. *Poems*, I, 17.

23. "Miss Lazarus's Translation of Heine," *Century*, 23 (March 1882), 785–86.

24. "The Poet Heine," *Century*, 29 (December 1884), 210–17.

Chapter Ten

1. *Letters to E. L.*, p. v.

2. E. C. Stedman, *Genius and other Essays* (1911; repr. Port Washington, N.Y., 1966), pp. 265–66.

3. Gustav Gottheil, *Hymns and Anthems adapted for Jewish Worship* (New York, 1889), number 46. See also Zeiger, p. 39, n. 20.

4. *Songs of a Semite: The Dance to Death and other Poems* (New York, 1882). All the poems and translations in this volume were reprinted in the 1889 *Poems*, volume 2, which will be the text cited here.

5. *E. L. Letters*, p. 48.

6. Another poem using a biblical theme is "Vashti," derived from the Book of Esther (*Independent*, May 4, 1876, p.1). The connection, however, is so tenuous that it needs no comment.

7. De Sola Pool, *Old Faith*, pp. 178, 181.

8. *New York Times*, October 8, 1882, p. 5.

9. Actually, the references to the harvest are more in keeping with the harvest holidays of Shavuot (Feast of Weeks) in the spring and of Succot (Tabernacles), which comes two weeks after Rosh Hashana. I do not think, however, that this displays an error on Lazarus's part, only a poetic transfer to Rosh Hashana.

10. Zeiger, p. 39, n. 23, and p. 41, n. 25, offers complete bibliographical background.

11. *E. L. Letters*, p. 20. See also Gottheil, *Life of Gustav Gottheil*, p. 62.

12. First printed in *Jewish Messenger*, February 14, 1879, p. 1, not collected into *Songs of a Semite* (unlike most of her other translations of Jewish poets): reprinted in *Poems*, II, 192.

13. *E. L. Letters*, p. 29.

14. July 27, 1881; *E. L. Letters*, p. 31.

15. In the *American Hebrew* for May 23, 1884; reprinted in *Century* the following month.

16. Heinrich Graetz, *Geschichte der Juden*, English lang. ed. [*History of the Jews*] (New York, 1927), III, 324, 325–26. That Lazarus knew Graetz's *Geschichte* is evident from the fact that in 1882 she identifies the source of her poem "An Epistle" by specific volume and page number in this history.

17. Both published in the *Independent*.

18. Zeiger, p. 55, n. 61, suggests Leopold Zunz's *Zeitschrift fur Wissenschaft des Judentum* (1816) as a source, as well as Karl Emil Franzos's *Jews of Barnow* (published as a series, 1868–74).

19. Albert Mordell, "The 100th Birthday of Emma Lazarus: July 22, 1849–November 19, 1887," *Jewish Book Annual: 1948–1949*, 7 (1949), 86.

20. Zeiger, p. 57.

21. *Ibid.*, p. 58.

Chapter Eleven

1. James Bryce, "*Lord Beaconsfield*," *Century*, 23 (March 1882), 729–44.

2. Quoted by Zeiger, p. 102.

3. "Was the Earl of Beaconsfield a Representative Jew?" *Century*, 23

(April 1882), 939–42.

4. Cyrus L. Sulzberger, "Was Beaconsfield a Representative Jew?" *American Hebrew*, March 31, 1882, p. 77. That the date of Sulzberger's rejoinder antedates Lazarus's essay is unusual, but not erroneous: the *Century* number for April was in the press in March and R. W. Gilder probably showed proofs of Lazarus's article to Sulzberger, whereupon he quickly penned his brief note for the *American Hebrew*, a weekly. Gilder did the same with Ragozin's article (see next section of this chapter), showing proof to Lazarus to stimulate response for the next issue.

5. *Ibid.*

6. Mme. Z. Ragozin, "Russian Jews and Gentiles," *Century*, 23 (April 1882), 906–20.

7. *Century*, 24 (May 1882), 48–56.

8. "The Jewish Problem," *Century*, 25 (February 1883), 602–11.

Chapter Twelve

1. New York, 1882.

2. Zeiger, p. 48.

3. *Lippincott's*, 31 (February 1883), 216.

4. *E. L. Letters*, p. 35.

5. See M. F. Modder, *The Jew in the Literature of England* (Philadelphia, 1944), pp. 253, 278–79. Lazarus may also have known about George Eliot's interest in Disraeli. Albert Mordell ("100th Birthday," p. 82), thinks Lazarus did not believe that conditions she dramatized would be repeated in her lifetime. This seems doubtful: while she was composing *The Dance to Death*, conditions in Europe were changing; hence, Eliot's essay in that year.

6. *Lippincott's*, 21 (February 1883), 216.

7. Quoted in "What They Say of Emma Lazarus [sic] Last Work," *American Hebrew*, October 14, 1882, p. 98.

8. Quoted, *ibid,*. January 5, 1883, p. 89.

9. *Critic*, 2 (November 1882), p. 267.

10. *Lippincott's, ibid.*; *Jewish Chronicle of London*, quoted in *American Hebrew*, November 17, 1882, p. 5; "A Tragedy of Persecution," *Jewish Messenger*, October 13, 1882, p. 4; *Critic*, 2 (November 1882), p. 267.

11. *New York Times*, October 8, 1882, p. 5.

12. Stedman, *Poets of America*, p. 447.

13. Mayer Sulzberger, "Miss Lazarus's Poems," *Jewish Messenger*, November 10, 1882, p. 5.

14. A useful codification of themes appears in Marc Dwight Angel, "The Jewish Poems of Emma Lazarus," *American Sephardi*, 2 (1968), 60–63. I am indebted to Mrs. E. Lubetski, Librarian of the Stern College Library, New York, for drawing my attention to this article.

15. *Lippincott's*, 31 (February 1883), 216.

16. Noted by the reviewer in *Lippincott's, ibid.*

17. Quoted by Murray Frank, "Emma Lazarus—Symbol of Liberty," *Chicago Jewish Forum*, 6 (Spring 1948), 254.

18. Quoted in "Miss Lazarus's 'Songs of a Semite,' " *American Hebrew*, January 5, 1883, p. 89.

19. The extremely religious among Oriental and East European Jews, in accordance with the biblical precept in Leviticus 19:27, affected long earlocks and beards.

20. Quoted in *American Hebrew*, January 5, 1883, p. 89.

21. Van Wyck Brooks, *The Times of Melville and Whitman* (New York, 1947), p. 316.

Chapter Thirteen

1. In "The Last National Revolt," in 1884, Lazarus again sees this enigmatic leader in a more positive light than some rabbinical authorities or than Ernst Renan, whose essay on the Jews she discussed in an article in this same year. See Zeiger, p. 180.

2. To Philip Cowen, May 5, 1883; *E. L. Letters*, p. 57.

3. *American Hebrew*, May 11, 1883. The translation, together with Alcharisi's Hebrew text, was printed in the *American Hebrew Memorial Issue*, p. 8.

4. See Max I. Baym, "A Neglected Translator of Italian Poetry; Emma Lazarus," *Italica*, 21 (December 1944), 175–85.

5. Zeiger, pp. 203, 205.

6. Obituary, *American Hebrew*, November 25, 1887, p. 35. It is an interesting historical oddity that in 1962 Charles Reznikoff published his own series of little poems in prose about the Jewish exile and called them "By the Waters of Manhattan." His concept of free verse is apparently similar to Lazarus's, as well.

7. This is the date appended to the manuscript text of "Venus of the Louvre," together with a note that it was printed in the *Century* in December 1884. The sonnet was the headnote to her essay on Heine. Kramer claims 1883 as the year of composition ("Links between Heinrich Heine and Emma Lazarus," p. 257).

8. Josephine Lazarus, *Poems*, I, 30.

9. *American Hebrew Memorial Issue*, p. 5.

10. *New Yorker*, 25 (July 23, 1949), quoted by Zeiger, p. 207. The lines were, however, set to music by Irving Berlin for his Broadway show, *Miss Liberty*.

11. *Letters to E. L.*, p. 74, dated "17 Decr 1883."

Chapter Fourteen

1. Abraham Cahan, *The Education of Abraham Cahan*, trans. Leon Stein, Abraham P. Conan, and Lynn Davison (Philadelphia, 1969), p. 354.

2. See Dan Vogel, "Cahan's *Rise of David Levinsky*: Archetype of American Jewish Fiction," *Judaism*, 22 (Summer 1973), 278–87.

3. Leslie Fiedler, "The Jew as Mythic American," *Ramparts*, 3 (Autumn 1963), 41.

Selected Bibliography

PRIMARY SOURCES

1. Collections of Poems in Lifetime
Admetus and Other Poems. New York: Hurd and Houghton, 1871.
Poems and Ballads of Heinrich Heine (translations with introduction). New York: R. Worthington, 1881.
Poems and Translations, Written between the Ages of Fourteen and Sixteen. New York: H. O. Houghton, 1867; second printing, Boston: Hurd and Houghton, 1867.
The Spagnoletto (verse drama). Private printing, 1876.
Songs of a Semite: The Dance to Death and Other Poems. New York: The American Hebrew, 1882.

2. Fiction
Alide, An Episode of Goethe's Life. Philadelphia: Lippincott, 1874.
"The Eleventh Hour," *Scribner's* [*Century*] 16 (June 1878), 252–56.

3. Letters
The Letters of Emma Lazarus, 1868–1885. Morris U. Schappes, ed. New York: New York Public Library, 1949.
Letters to Emma Lazarus in the Columbia University Library. Ralph L. Rusk, ed. New York: Columbia University Library, 1939.
Letters from Henry James to Emma a Lazarus (in manuscript). Columbia University Library, New York.
"An Unpublished Emma Lazarus Letter," Samuel Golden, ed., *Boston Public Library Quarterly*, 10 (1958), 54–55.

4. Manuscripts
Manuscript Notebook. Library of the American Jewish Historical Society, Waltham, Mass. Fair copies of a number of published and unpublished poems.

5. Posthumous Collections
The Poems of Emma Lazarus. 2 vols. Boston: Houghton, Mifflin and Co., 1889./Vol. I: poems first printed in popular magazines; vol. II: Jewish poems and miscellaneous translations. *Not* a complete collection.

An Epistle to the Hebrews. New York: Federation of American Zionists, 1900. Gathering of essays printed serially under this title in 1882–83.

MORRIS U. SCHAPPES, ed. *Emma Lazarus. Selections from Her Poetry and Prose*. New York: Co-operative Book League, 1944. "Revised and Enlarged." New York: Emma Lazarus Federation of Jewish Women's Clubs, 1967. With introduction and notes.

6. Uncollected Materials

A. *Poetry in Print*

In *Lippincott's Magazine*:

"Carmela," XVI (December 1875), 689–91.

"Changes," XII (July 1873), 116–17.

"The Christmas Tree," XIX (February 1877), 229–30.

"Dolores," XVII (June 1876), 666–67.

"Expectation," XI (November 1872), 587–88.

"Fra Aloysius," XVII (February 1876), 183–84.

"La Madonna Della Sedia: A Tradition," XV (March 1875), 334–37.

"A March Violet," XV (April 1875), 481–82.

"Moods," XVI (September 1875), 283.

"Neighborly Love", XXII (October 1878), 507.

"Phantasmagoria," XVIII (August 1876), 157–58.

"Prothalamion," XIX (June 1877), 707.

"Rosemary," IX (May 1872), 542–43.

"Reverie," XIV (December 1874), 722.

"The Sacrifice," X (August 1872), 162.

"Scenes in the Wood (Suggested by Robert Schuman)," XVI (August 1875), 175–78.

"Similitude: From Goethe," XII (October 1873), 438.

"Spring (After a Picture by A. Cot), Translated from the French of Francois Coppè," XIX (May 1877), 578–79.

"Spring Joy" XV (May 1875), 570.

"Translations from the French of Francois Coppè," XIX (January 1877), 25–26.

"Teresa Di Faenza," XXVI (July 1880), 83.

"Three Friends," XXIV (November 1879), 615–16.

"Under the Sea," XVIII (October 1876), 476.

"Will o' the Wisp," XIX (April 1877), 465.

"The Winds," XVI (October 1875), 438–40.

"Winter Night," XXI (March 1878), 376.

In Other Magazines

"Among the Thousand Islands," *Century*, XXIII (December 1881), 288–89.

"Comoedia," *Independent*, XXIX, No. 1495 (July 26, 1877), 1.

"Consolation. Translated from the Hebrew." *American Hebrew*, XIV, No.

13 (May 11, 1883), 147.

"Grotesque," *Galaxy*, XXIV (December 1877), 770–71.

"Moses Maimonides, an unrhymed Ballad," *American Hebrew*, XX (September 12, 1884), 72.

"Outside the Church," *Index*, III (December 1872), 399.

"Progress and Poverty" *New York Times*, October 2, 1881, 2.

"The Taming of the Falcon," *Century*, XXI (December 1879), 196.

"To R. W. E." *Critic*, IV (August 1884), 5–6.

"Vashti" *Independent*, XXVIII (May 4, 1876), 1.

"Zuleika", *Jewish Messenger*, XLIV, No. 14 (October 4, 1876), 1.

7. Unpublished Poetry in Manuscript

"Ariel and Euphoron," clippings of printed copy pasted into notebook, journal not named, n.d., leaves 120–21.

"Art the Redeemer," dated January 2, 1881, leaf 41.

"Assurance", n.d., leaf 19.

"Child at the Bath. R. de K. G.", dated March 22, 1881, leaves 53–54.

"The Creation of Man. Miwk [Mohawk] Fable," dated February 1879, leaves 89–97.

"Dreaming-Castle. To S. G. W. & A. B. W.", dated July 22, 1880, leaf 28.

"From the Arabian Nights," n.d., leaf 57.

"In a Gothic Church" (never completed), n.d., leaves 161–63.

"Lida & the Swan. Faust. Part II. Act II. Scene 2," dated January 1878, leaf 61.

"Moonlight, from German of Eichendorff," n.d., leaf 59.

"My Goddess. From the German of Goethe," n.d., leaves 112–15.

"The New Cupid. From the German of Goethe," dated "1873–4," leaves 98–105.

"The Old Year—1883. Affectionately dedicated to W. S. P. & W. A. P.," dated December 29, 1883, leaves 116–19.

"Phaon," dated November 1877, leaves 62–72.

"Reconciliation," dated July 6, 1879, leaf 16.

"Reed Song," dated "1877," leaf 58.

"Songs from Eichendorff," n.d., leaf 60.

"Sympathy," n.d., leaf 27.

"To F. P.," dated May 1882, leaf 13.

"To the Moon after Sunrise," dated February 1881, leaf 73.

"To Nelly [?] Sleeping," dated July 24, 1878, leaves 85–88.

"To — With a Copy of Don Quixote," dated "Christmas 1881," leaf 12.

"Translations from Coppè," n.d., leaves 131–36.

8. Essays and Reviews

"American Literature," *Critic*, I (June 1882), 164.

"A Bit of British Impudence," *American Hebrew*, XIV (May 25, 1883), 14.

"Bernay as Mark Antony," *Century*, XXVI (June 1883), 312.

"Cruel Bigotry," *American Hebrew*, XIV (May 25, 1883), 14.

"A Day in Surrey with William Morris," *Century*, XXXII (July 1886), 388–97.

"Emerson's Personality," *Century*, XXIV (June 1882), 454–55.

"Eugene Fromentin," *Critic*, I (December 1881), 364–65.

"Henry Wadsworth Longfellow," *American Hebrew*, XI (April 14, 1882), 98–99.

"J. A. Symonds' *Sketches and Studies in Southern Europe*," *Jewish Messenger*, XLVII (June 25, 1880), 4–5.

"The Jewish Problem," *Century*, XXV (February 1883), 602–11.

"Joseffy," *Musical Review*, I (November 1879), 51–52.

"Judaism the Connecting Link between Science and Religion," *American Hebrew*, XII (September 1, 1882), 28.

"The Last National Revolt of the Jews," *American Hebrew*, XXI (November 14, 21, 28, 1884), 2–4, 24–25, 34–35.

"M. Renan and the Jews," *American Hebrew*, XX (October 24, 1884), 163–64.

"The Poet Heine," *Century*, XXIX (December 1884), 210–17.

"Regnault as a Writer," *Critic*, I (February 1881), 37.

"Russian Christianity versus Modern Judaism," *Century*, XXIV (May 1882), 48–56.

"Salvini's King Lear," *Century*, XXVI (May 1883), 89–91.

"The Schiff Refuge," *American Hebrew*, XII (October 20, 1882), 114–15.

"Tommaso Salvini," *Century*, XXIII (November 1881), 110–17.

"Was the Earl of Beaconsfield a Representative Jew?" *Century*, XXIII (April 1882), 939–42.

SECONDARY SOURCES

BAYM, MAX I. "Emma Lazarus and Emerson," *Publications of the American Jewish Historical Society*, XXXVIII (1949), 261–87. Detailed documentation of their relationship, marred by Baym's weakly-supported conjecture that had Lazarus been represented in *Parnassus*, she would never have had a "Jewish phase."

_____. "Emma Lazarus' Approach to Renan in her essay 'Renan and the Jews,' " *Publications of the American Jewish Historical Society*, XXXVII (1947), 17–29. Shows Lazarus's naiveté in analyzing a non-Jew's attitude.

_____. "A Neglected Translator of Italian Poetry: Emma Lazarus," *Italica*, XXI (December 1944), 175–85. A fine, thorough, and judicious discussion of Lazarus's translations of Petrarch.

COWEN, PHILIP. "Emma Lazarus," in Harold U. Ribalow, ed., *Autobiographies of American Jews* (Philadelphia; Jewish Publication Society of America, 1968), pp. 27–37. An objective, but sympathetic, sketch by a contemporary, the editor of the *American Hebrew*.

HARAP, LOUIS. *The Image of the Jew in American Literature: From Early*

    Republic to Mass Immigration (Philadelphia: The Jewish Publication
  Society of America, 1974), pp. 284–99. The best introductory essay yet
  published.

JACOB, H. E. *The World of Emma Lazarus* (New York: Schocken, 1949).
  Romanticized, Freudianized biography, making Emma into Electra.

KAZIN, ALFRED. "The Jew as Modern Writer," *Commentary*, XLI (April 1966),
  37–41. Important in that this eminent critic places Lazarus in the
  mainstream of American-Jewish literature.

LAZARUS, JOSEPHINE. "Emma Lazarus," in *Poems of Emma Lazarus* (Boston:
  Houghton-Mifflin, 1889). Indispensable, if sisterly, memoir.

MORDELL, ALBERT. "The 100th Birthday of Emma Lazarus: July 22, 1849–
  November 19, 1887," *Jewish Book Annual: 1948–1949*, VII (1949), pp.
  79–88. Disputes Baym's conjecture about Lazarus's Jewish phase.

————. "Some Final Words on Emma Lazarus," *Publications of American
  Jewish Historical Society*, XXXIX (1950), 321–27. Controverts Baym's
  analysis of Lazarus's interpretation of Renan.

————. "Some Neglected Phases of Emma Lazarus' Genius," *Jewish
  Forum*, XXXII (October 1949), 181–82,·187. Centenary essay, tending
  toward Freudian interpretation of poems of early 1870s.

ROSENFELD, GERALDINE. Emma Lazarus and Heinrich Heine. Unpubl. master's essay. Columbia University, 1939. Thorough thematic and technical study.

RUCHAMES, LOUIS. "New Light on the Religious Development of Emma
  Lazarus," *Publications of American Historical Society*, XLII (1952), 83–
  88. On "Outside the Church." Very informative, but overstated.

ZEIGER, ARTHUR. *Emma Lazarus: A Critical Study.* Unpubl. Ph.D. dissertation. New York University, 1952. Thorough, but unsympathetic in
  interpretation and evaluation. Secondary bibliography excellent to its
  date.

Index

179

811.4
L431

110 294